CONFLICT OR CODETERMINATION?

CONFLICT OR CODETERMINATION?
Congress, the President, and the Power to Make War

MARC E. SMYRL

A Defense Forecasts Book

Ballinger Publishing Company
Cambridge, Massachusetts
A Subsidiary of Harper & Row, Publishers, Inc.

The research for this book was undertaken as part of a larger study of the Congress and Defense Policy. That research was funded in part by the Twentieth Century Fund. Mr. Smyrl is grateful to the fund for its support but wishes to make clear that the opinions in the book are entirely his own and not necessarily endorsed by that organization.

Copyright © 1988 by Ballinger Publishing Company. All rights reserved. No part of this publication may be reproduced, stored in a retrieval system, or transmitted in any form or by any means, electronic, mechanical, photocopy, recording or otherwise, without the prior written consent of the publisher.

International Standard Book Number: 0-88730-310-2

Library of Congress Catalog Card Number: 88-19237

Printed in the United States of America

Library of Congress Cataloging-in-Publication Data

Smyrl, Marc E., 1960–
   Conflict or codetermination?

  "A Defense Forecasts Inc. book."
  Includes index.
  1. War and emergency powers—United States.
2. Executive power—United States. 3. Legislative power—United States. I. Title.
KF5060.S571988342.73'05288–19237
ISBN 0-88730-310-2347.30252

CONTENTS

Foreword
Barry M. Blechman — vii

Introduction — xi

PART I   **FROM PRESIDENTIAL SUPREMACY TO CONGRESSIONAL "REVOLUTION"** — 1

Chapter 1   **A Zone of Twilight** — 3
- The Problem of War Powers — 4
- Constitutional Ambiguity — 5
- Twentieth-Century Trends and Developments — 8
- Congress Defines Its War Powers — 10
- Moves against the Vietnam War — 13

Chapter 2   **The War Powers Resolution** — 19
- Initial War Powers Proposals — 19
- Passage of the War Powers Resolution — 23
- Provisions of the War Powers Resolution — 26
- Conclusion: The WPR in Perspective — 28

Chapter 3   **Revolution or Lost Opportunities?** — 31
- Problems of Scope and Constitutionality — 32
- The Early Record of Implementation — 37
- Motives and Strategies — 45

	Congress and Foreign Policy in the 1970s: A Broader View	51
	Conclusion: The Politics of War Powers in the 1970s	57
PART II	**TOWARD A NEW EQUILIBRIUM**	61
Chapter 4	**Presidential Initiatives**	63
	Theoretical Considerations	65
	Brief Military Operations: Grenada and Libya	69
	Prolonged Low-level Military Presence: Central America	81
	Purse-string Restrictions in Central America	90
	The Power of Persuasion	95
Chapter 5	**Congress Defends Its Gains**	97
	U.S. Participation in the Beirut Multinational Force	97
	The Reagan Administration and the Nicaraguan Contras	117
Chapter 6	**The Collective Judgment of Congress and the President**	127
	The Power to Make War: The Status Quo in 1987	128
	Directions for the Future	140

Appendix
Text of the War Powers Resolution 153

Notes 161

Index 175

About the Author 181

FOREWORD

War powers, the authority to commit American armed forces to combat or to deploy them in hostile situations implying a significant risk of combat, have been an enduring source of conflict between the Legislative and Executive branches virtually throughout the history of the Republic. In recent years, the issue was debated most pointedly in the context of the war in Indochina and was ostensibly set to rest—once and for all—with the passage over President Nixon's veto of the War Powers Resolution, which made clear the perogatives of the Congress regarding commitments of American forces in situations short of formal wars.

Yet, as Marc Smyrl makes clear in this book, every President since Richard Nixon, Republican and Democrat alike, has carefully avoided officially recognizing the legitimacy of key provisions of the War Powers Resolution. Moreover, the Legislature itself, particularly the Senate, has been divided over both the political wisdom and legitimacy of the powers that the 93d Congress assumed in passing the resolution in 1973.

These issues once again came to a head as the United States became more deeply involved militarily in the Persian Gulf. In 1987 President Reagan unilaterally committed American naval forces into what was obviously a combat situation, acting on the belief that his constitutional authority as commander-in-chief gives the President the right to assume nearly total responsibility for the direction—including the initiation—of

U.S. military activities abroad. A large number of Senators and Members of Congress, however, including key members of the President's own party, disputed these actions, claiming that the Congress had the right to participate in any decision threatening to involve American troops in the modern-day version of war. Some Representatives took the issue to the courts, seeking a judicial order to stay the President's hand. Others, in both Houses, hoped to implement key provisions of the War Powers Resolution that would limit the length of time American forces could remain in the Persian Gulf without congressional approval.

Neither action has proven effective. The courts have consistently refused to become involved in this constitutional struggle between the two other branches, while enough legislators have doubted the political utility, if not the legitimacy, of a congressional initiative to prevent implementation of the War Powers Resolution, and thus to avoid a constitutional confrontation.

Indeed, the one point upon which the Congress seems able to agree is that the resolution should be rewritten. A special panel of the Senate Foreign Relations Committee has been created to review the legislation. The panel will consider specific amendments to the War Powers Resolution contained in draft legislation introduced by Senate Majority Leader Robert Byrd and others in May 1988, and will likely explore other possibilities as well. Some Members have called for the creation of a bipartisan Executive-Legislative commission to consider the issue. While the press of business in an election year makes it unlikely that much progress will be made in 1988, the question of war powers may well turn out to be one of the priorities of the 101st Congress. *Conflict or Codetermination?* is thus a timely contribution to our understanding of war powers and the debate over the relative authority of the two branches of government in their implementation.

This book traces congressional efforts to assert influence in warmaking decisions from the late 1960s to the present. Smyrl analyzes the goals, motives, and methods of both the proponents and opponents of the 1973 legislation and provides a detailed legislative history. He goes on to recount the record of its implementation, from minor incidents during the Ford and Carter Administrations to the Reagan Administration's 1987 Persian Gulf operations. Smyrl also examines other means through which Members of Congress have sought to influence commitments of forces abroad, including attempts to utilize the "power of the purse" to curtail military activities in Southeast Asia, southern Africa, and Central America.

Smyrl concludes that the War Powers Resolution, on balance, has been a positive achievement, helping to ensure a congressional role in crucial issues of war and peace. Most important, he notes, the resolution serves as an institutionalized reminder of the dangers inherent in piecemeal, open-ended commitments of forces abroad, such as those that engaged the United States ever more deeply in the conflict in Vietnam. This is not to say, however, that the resolution has fulfilled all its objectives and could not be improved. Thus Smyrl offers specific suggestions for tying the Congress' disputed power to oversee military operations more closely to its uncontested power to appropriate monies, and for reconsidering some of the resolution's "automatic" provisions, which have been challenged on constitutional grounds and which, in any case, have proven unworkable in practice.

Defense Forecasts, Inc. is a research and analysis enterprise in Washington, D.C., specializing in political/military issues and defense budget analyses. Our clients include government agencies, foundations, and private organizations. We are pleased to have sponsored this research, and we present it in the interest of stimulating more informed public debate on this important issue.

Barry M. Blechman, President
Defense Forecasts, Inc.

INTRODUCTION

The unprecedented increase in the size of the U.S. naval force in the Persian Gulf following the 1987 U.S. decision to provide naval escorts for Kuwaiti oil tankers re-registered under the U.S. flag, and the ensuing clashes with Iranian forces, renewed attention to the President's power to commit U.S. armed forces to missions involving a high risk of hostility. Only a few months previously, on May 17, 1987, the Iraqui attack on the frigate *U.S.S. Stark* had cost the lives of thirty-seven American servicemen—a tragic reminder of the possible cost of such commitments.

These incidents in the Persian Gulf were not isolated occurrences. A number of events throughout the 1980s, ranging from naval exercises in the Mediterranean to the invasion of Grenada, highlighted other aspects of the complex problem of war powers. Is the decision to employ U.S. armed forces abroad one that the President may properly make alone? To what extent does a presidential decision, or even public announcement, constitute a formal commitment by the U.S. Government? Do Members of Congress have a legitimate role in the policymaking process leading to such a decision? What recourse might the Legislative branch have if the Administration does not willingly include Congress in its decision-making?

Revelations, in 1986 and 1987, of Executive branch actions in Nicaragua suggest a related set of questions. Can Congress legitimately control the scope and direction of covert military activities? Can it reasonably expect to succeed in attempts to do so? To what extent are the President and his personal advisors bound by congressionally mandated restrictions? What are the limits of congressional control over the U.S. Government's purse strings?

Behind all of these questions lies a broader issue: is it in the best interest of the United States for crucial foreign policy decisions to be subject to congressional scrutiny and criticism? This is the fundamental question that must be answered.

These issues are not new. Two hundred years after the drafting of the U.S. Constitution, the question of war powers remains one of the most contentious issues involving American government and the constitutional process. U.S. history yields contradictory examples and precedents on this question. At various times, both Congresses and Presidents have taken the lead on foreign policy issues. At other times, the two have acted in concert; occasionally they have been in open conflict.

By the latter half of the twentieth century, the Executive branch had become the dominant force in U.S. foreign and military policy. From Franklin D. Roosevelt through Richard Nixon, Presidents exercised virtually complete authority over all questions regarding the use of U.S. armed forces, both open and covert. Beginning in the 1960s, however, this status quo was increasingly challenged by Members of Congress, and eventually by the Legislative branch as a whole.

The passage of the War Powers Resolution of 1973 is the best known symbol of a congressional desire to assert greater influence in formulating U.S. foreign policy, especially concerning the actual or potential use of U.S. armed forces. This sentiment was also manifested in legislative efforts to limit the use of U.S. armed forces in particular cases. Although these initiatives—particularly the War Powers Resolution—have met with mixed results, since the late 1960s, relative institutional power and Executive behavior has undergone a significant shift.

The contrast between the degree of congressional oversight exercised during the 1970s and 1980s and that exercised from 1945 through the early 1960s is striking. From Angola in the 1970s to Lebanon and Nicaragua in the 1980s, the Congress repeatedly demonstrated an ability to limit, or even to reverse, Executive initiatives taken without its consent, if only when such acts proved politically unpopular.

This shift was due largely to a significant increase in the level and extent of public debate on questions of military involvement overseas, an obvious political legacy of the Vietnam War. By encouraginging Members of Congress to challenge the President's stand on certain foreign policy issues, the new public attitude ensured continued legislative participation in foreign affairs decision-making and presaged further policy reversals if the Executive branch failed to adapt to the expanded legislative role.

Indeed, this role has increasingly influenced the Executive branch. The actual policies followed by the Reagan Administration, as distinguished from the public rhetoric of its spokesmen, suggest that the Executive branch may be coming to recognize the practical limits that the Congress now places on its freedom of action. It is remarkable, in retrospect, that an Administration whose publicly stated foreign policy positions and objectives have been more aggressive than any others in recent memory has been relatively cautious in its actions when compared to Administrations in previous decades.

This book examines the evolution of Congress' role in war powers questions from the Vietnam War through 1987. At the heart of the analysis is a detailed study of the War Powers Resolution of 1973. Part I traces historical trends and patterns of Legislative-Executive relations on the issue of war powers. Beginning with a brief exposition of the rise of presidential power, we move to a detailed study of the legislative history of the War Powers Resolution, the circumstances of its passage, and the early record of its implementation. To ensure a sense of perspective, we also examine and contrast the results of parallel congressional efforts to influence foreign policy, from the funding restrictions that ended U.S. involvement in Southeast Asia to attempts in the late 1970s to influence such activities as arms sales and intelligence.

In the second section, we seek to determine whether a new, more stable status quo has emerged over the course of the Reagan Administration. By analyzing and contrasting those cases in which the President has been able to act without significant congressional opposition with others, such as the longstanding Nicaraguan debate and the issues surrounding the presence of U.S. Marines in Beirut from 1982 to 1984, in which the Administration has encountered strong and effective congressional opposition, we explore the nature and limits of the post-Vietnam balance of power between the Executive and Legislative branches.

This study is approached throughout from the perspective of the Congress. Primary sources consulted in writing the book include legislative texts such as bills and committee reports, the debates recorded in hearing transcripts and the *Congressional Record,* and documentation from the Congressional Research Service and the General Accounting Office. The writings and public statements of present and former Members of Congress provide another fruitful source of material for this history. Contemporary press accounts, finally, define the larger context within which congressional actions and debates took place.

These materials constitute the public record of Congress' goals, actions, and intentions, as well as the principal information sources available to congressional decision-makers themselves. By examining and analyzing this information, we hope to clarify the motives and expectations of the diverse individuals and coalitions that make up the U.S. Congress and assess the extent to which the Legislative branch has been successful in implementing its self-defined goals.

CONFLICT OR CODETERMINATION?

FROM PRESIDENTIAL SUPREMACY TO CONGRESSIONAL "REVOLUTION"

1 A ZONE OF TWILIGHT

On October 21, 1987, the U.S. Senate approved by a vote of 54 to 44 a joint resolution (S.J. Res. 194, 100th Cong.) requiring the President to submit to Congress within thirty days of the measure's enactment a formal report detailing the goals, methods, and costs of the activities undertaken by U.S. naval forces in the Persian Gulf.[1] The resolution also mandated that within thirty days of the receipt of this report, the Congress would take further, unspecified action on the Persian Gulf question.

Although it eventually passed by a comfortable margin, the resolution had faced considerable opposition in the Senate, defeated by a vote of 47 to 51 in an initial vote, with opposition coming from both ends of the political spectrum. Only after parliamentary maneuvering and forceful persuasion by the Senate Majority Leader was the measure reconsidered and finally passed.[2]

At first glance, this controversy seemed entirely out of proportion to the measure itself. Requests for presidential reports are made not infrequently by both Houses of Congress and are often uncontentious. The resolution of October 21, however, was passed only after more than a month of often bitter debate, over the course of which a number of legislative options were considered, and whose progress was frequently interrupted by some conservative Senators' delaying tactics.

THE PROBLEM OF WAR POWERS

The explanation for this heated and prolonged controversy lies in the larger context of the issue. At the heart of the 1987 debate was not the resolution that was finally passed—a carefully worded compromise with little immediate effect—but another, far more significant piece of legislation: the War Powers Resolution of 1973 (WPR). Whether or not to invoke the WPR in the context of the U.S. involvement in the Persian Gulf was a question that divided both the Senate and the Congress as a whole, cutting across party lines and generating intense passion on both sides of the issue.

Many Senators, led by Mark Hatfield (R-OR) and Lowell Weicker (R-CT), believed that the situation in the Gulf, coupled with the increasing U.S. involvement in this volatile region, compelled the Congress to act under the WPR. To do otherwise, they claimed, would forfeit any opportunity for effective congressional participation in decision-making regarding present or future U.S. actions in the Gulf. The Reagan Administration was equally adamant on the other side of the issue. The President and his spokesmen issued repeated warnings to the Congress, claiming that any move to invoke the War Powers Resolution would undermine American policy in the Gulf and harm the national interest of the United States.[3]

The October 21 Senate resolution sought a common ground among these contending points of view. Sponsored by Senate Majority Leader Robert Byrd (D-WV) and Senator John Warner (R-VA), it mentioned the WPR only to note that nothing within the Byrd-Warner resolution should be construed as modifying or negating the WPR. By requiring a presidential report and providing for congressional action to follow, the Byrd-Warner resolution did, to a certain extent, mirror some provisions of the WPR. The 1987 measure, however, stopped far short of the mandatory and automatic stipulations of the 1973 law, the best known—and most controversial—of which mandated that U.S. military initiatives end within ninety days unless expressly approved by Congress.

Passage of the Byrd-Warner resolution brought a momentary halt to the Persian Gulf debate. The broader issue of war powers, however, was not clarified by this exercise. Indeed, over the course of the debates on the Gulf, it became apparent that considerable confusion existed within the

Congress itself as to what the actual effect of invoking the WPR might be. Certain Members saw the WPR principally as a means of ensuring that the Congress would be consulted and informed, and even as a vehicle by which it could express formal support for the President's policy; others seemed eager to use it as a means of reversing the Administration's initiatives. For some, invoking the WPR represented unwarranted congressional meddling in matters that were properly the province of the Executive branch, and risked sparking a constitutional conflict between Congress and the President.

The precise definition of the relative war powers of the Executive and Legislative branches has long been a topic of considerable controversy, not only between the branches but within them. The legislative text at issue in the Persian Gulf debate, the WPR, represented Congress' most ambitious attempt to define its war powers—an attempt that, as shown here, was less than fully successful. It was a direct product of the political reaction to the American experience in Vietnam, a heritage that imbued the resolution with an important symbolic and emotional dimension. The broader question of war powers, however, dated back to the founding of the American Republic.

Thus, to understand the significance and context of the debate over war powers as it was waged in the 1980s, we must return to the origins of the issue. These are found most directly in the politics and controversies of the late 1960s and early 1970s, centered on the bitter and protracted struggle over American policy in Vietnam. The conduct of U.S. policy in Vietnam was the culmination of a trend in American government, visible since the early years of the twentieth century, toward ever greater presidential control of U.S. foreign and military policy. This in turn occurred because the fundamental principles of American government, beginning with the U.S. Constitution, proved to be less than clear on this question. It is with this problem of constitutional intent that we begin our exploration of the war powers issue.

CONSTITUTIONAL AMBIGUITY

The Constitution of the United States divided authority over military activities between the Executive and Legislative branches of government.

The President, in addition to being vested with the executive powers of government, was named commander-in-chief of the armed forces and empowered to make treaties (subject to Senate ratification) and to "name and receive ambassadors," implying the discretionary authority to extend or deny official recognition to foreign governments and, more broadly, to carry out diplomacy (U.S. Constitution: Art. 2).

The Congress, for its part, was given the power "to raise and support armies . . . to provide and maintain a navy . . . [and] to make rules for the government and regulation of the land and naval forces." The power of Congress to declare war is well known. Significantly, Congress was empowered in addition to "grant letters of Marque and Reprisal . . . [and] to define and punish piracies and felonies committed on the high seas and offenses against the laws of nations," powers that clearly apply in the absence of a formal declaration of war (U.S. Constitution: Art. 1).

This divided authority represented a significant departure from the general practice of the time, in which military power was almost universally vested in the Executive. It was a step back, nevertheless, from the earlier Articles of Confederation, which had vested all executive power in a single representative body. Clearly, the delegates to the Philadelphia Convention sought a middle ground between these two extremes. Their compromise, however, created ambiguities that persist to this day.

The record of the Constitutional Convention itself is not particularly helpful in this context. Despite the scope of the change that was proposed, the subject of war powers was not debated extensively at the convention. The only documented change the delegates made to the draft was an amendment proposed by James Madison and Elbridge Gerry that gave Congress the power to "declare war" rather than "make war," as stated in the original draft. Madison's notes, taken at the time, make it clear that he intended this change to ensure that, while the initiation of hostilities would be the prerogative of Congress, the President would retain the power to repel sudden attacks.[4]

Only a few years after ratification of the Constitution, however, Madison and Alexander Hamilton (both of whom had been delegates to the Philadelphia Convention) disagreed openly on the distribution of war powers. During the public debate following President Washington's Neutrality Proclamation of 1793, Madison reiterated his earlier claim that the Constitution defined decisions on war and peace as a legislative function, subject only to specific exceptions of which the most important was the President's limited authority as commander-in-chief. Hamilton made the opposite case, holding war-making to be an inherently Executive function, as exemplified by the traditional prerogatives of the British monarch. By granting certain powers to Congress, the Constitution defined specific exceptions to this rule but did not overturn it. Accordingly, Hamilton argued, these exceptions should be interpreted as narrowly as possible.[5] With remarkably few changes, this debate persists to the present day.

The case that the framers of the Constitution intended that Congress, rather than the President, should have the power to initiate the use of armed force is powerful nonetheless. Thomas Jefferson, writing to Madison in 1789, unequivocally stated, "We have already given in example one effectual check to the dog of war by transferring the power to let him loose from the Executive to the Legislative Body, from those who are to spend to those who are to pay."[6]

A look at the historical record, however, suggests that the ghost of Alexander Hamilton has carried the day more often than not. On numerous occasions, Presidents have initiated military actions on their own authority, without consulting the Congress. The Congressional Research Service has documented some 200 instances of the use of U.S. armed forces abroad between 1798 and 1983, of which only four (the War of 1812, the Spanish-American War, and the two world wars) were preceded by a formal Declaration of War, while one (the Mexican War of 1845) was authorized by a Joint Resolution of Congress.[7] Other compilations, such as one prepared by Senator Barry Goldwater (R-AZ) in 1973, include even more examples of presidentially initiated conflicts.[8]

These facts are not disputed. The continuing issue is that which Hamilton and Madison debated, namely the wisdom and legality of such presidential initiatives. This ongoing debate, and the various positions taken by successive presidents and legislators, led Supreme Court Justice Robert H. Jackson, in his 1952 opinion on President Truman's seizure of the steel industry during the Korean War, to observe that a "zone of twilight" existed between the discrete areas of presidential and congressional power in this matter.[9] Since the founding of the Republic, Congresses and

Presidents have both exploited this "constitutional twilight zone." From the early twentieth century, however, the tendency toward ever greater presidential power has grown.

TWENTIETH-CENTURY TRENDS AND DEVELOPMENTS

Certain presidentially initiated uses of military power during the nineteenth century created sharp controversy and had far-reaching consequences, such as the 1816 and 1817 expeditions into Spanish Florida that led to the U.S. acquisition of that territory. The vast majority, however, were for minor incidents concerning the pursuit of pirates or slave traders, or the defense of Americans in primitive areas of the world. None led to prolonged fighting or significant casualties.

The use of military force against sovereign nations became more common in the early twentieth century as Presidents Roosevelt, Taft, and Wilson undertook initiatives in China and, especially, Latin America, to protect American citizens and property, or more generally to uphold U.S. interests. This practice culminated in General Pershing's 1915–17 campaign in northern Mexico. Isolationist sentiment resurfaced in Congress following World War I, but did not prevent Presidents Coolidge and Hoover from employing U.S. troops to protect U.S. interests in Central America. None of these moves received serious congressional challenge, nor, however, were they accompanied by sweeping presidential assertions of a general or inherent power to make war.[10]

Both the scope of presidentially initiated conflicts and the legal powers claimed by the Executive changed radically after World War II. In 1950 President Truman ordered U.S. troops into a major conflict in Korea entirely on his own authority, without seeking any form of congressional authorization, let alone a formal declaration of war. The late Senator Jacob Javits (R-NY), in his book *Who Makes War*, describes the extent of the power claimed by the President on this occasion:

> Less than a week after the President had ordered American troops into Korea, the State Department was ready with an official memorandum "directed at the authority of the President of the United States to repel the aggressive attack on the Republic of Korea." According to the State Department, *the Presi-*

dent's authority as commander-in-chief was unlimited. The document asserted that he was authorized to send troops into combat "without Congressional authorization" in pursuit of his constitutional authority to conduct foreign affairs. (emphasis in original)[11]

The overwhelming bipartisan consensus on foreign policy that grew out of World War II and extended to the Cold War ensured that Congress raised no serious challenge to President Truman's action.

During the Eisenhower Administration, this continuing consensus led to the passage of broadly worded resolutions authorizing the President to take whatever measures he considered necessary—explicitly including the use of armed forces—to resist Communist aggression in Formosa and the Middle East. In seeking these resolutions, President Eisenhower emphasized that while he valued congressional support and wished to demonstrate the unified stand of the U.S. Government to foreign powers, his request for congressional declarations did not imply that he would have lacked constitutional authority to act in their absence.[12] Accordingly, Eisenhower neither cited the Middle East Resolution nor sought additional congressional authority when he dispatched U.S. troops to Lebanon in 1958.

The Kennedy Administration saw the passage of similar resolutions authorizing the President to take action in case of crises in Cuba or Berlin. In 1962 Kennedy demonstrated the continued power of the President by sending some 17,000 U.S. military advisors into South Vietnam. Three years later, President Johnson sent more than 20,000 U.S. troops to the Dominican Republic. Neither move was authorized by Congress, but again neither was challenged.

The now infamous Gulf of Tonkin Resolution, requested by President Johnson in 1964, followed the pattern of the earlier resolutions. Like President Eisenhower, Johnson took pains to indicate that he sought confirmation of his inherent powers, not the grant of exceptional authority.[13] The Tonkin Resolution passed unanimously in the House of Representatives and drew only two dissenting votes, Senators Wayne Morse (D-OR) and Ernest Gruening (D-AK), in the Senate. Thus the Truman Administration's claims remained intact—and largely unchallenged. Justice Jackson's "twilight zone," in the words of Senator Javits, had become "a kind of Constitutional DMZ, infiltrated by expansionist-minded Presidents."[14]

CONGRESS DEFINES ITS WAR POWERS

The Gulf of Tonkin Resolution heralded the beginning of a long, costly, and in the end, widely unpopular war. In this context, thoughtful observers both in and out of Congress concluded that the virtually unlimited war-making powers claimed and wielded by successive Presidents and uncontested by Congress were a major cause of the Vietnam debacle, as well as a potential source of similar disasters in the future. Accordingly, efforts were initiated by Members of Congress in the late 1960s to find means to ensure greater legislative participation in all phases of war-making.

Moves of this sort were not entirely without precedent. Although they constituted a small minority at the time, certain Members had expressed concerns over the delegation of congressional war powers implied by such security treaties as NATO and SEATO, which seemed to provide that U.S. troops would be automatically committed to defend foreign countries. In its 1949 report on the North Atlantic Treaty, the Senate Foreign Relations Committee explicitly asserted that the treaty gave the President no war-making powers that he did not previously possess, although it declined to spell out exactly what those previously held powers entailed.[15]

Congress' desire to impose some measure of accountability on the Executive—but also its continued reluctance to address the issue of war powers directly—was again borne out in the 1957 debate over the Middle East Resolution. Because of concerns in the Senate, language was added to the resolution requiring itemized periodic accounting of money spent on military assistance pursuant to the resolution's goals, and declaring that the President would be considered responsible for any hostilities in which the United States engaged under the so-called Eisenhower Doctrine. In the opinion of Senator Javits, these provisions marked "the first time since the end of WW 2 [that] Congress attempted at least to put some kind of limit on executive action that might lead to armed conflict."[16] On the other hand, the Middle East Resolution, unlike the Formosa Resolution, did not "authorize" the President to use armed force, but rather stated that "if the President determines the necessity thereof, the United States is prepared to use armed force. . . ." This language represented a further retreat from an attempt to define the division of war powers.[17]

President Johnson's escalation of U.S. intervention in Vietnam led to a gradual but profound change in congressional attitudes. In 1967, ten years after passage of the Middle East Resolution, and only three after that of the Gulf of Tonkin Resolution, the Senate took up the non-binding National Commitments Resolution, the first piece of legislation expressly intended to define, at least in part, the role that the Senate felt it should be playing in decisions on war and peace.

The National Commitments Resolution, which the Senate passed in 1969, was largely a reaction of the Senate Foreign Relations Committee to the Johnson Administration's repeated references to the U.S. "commitment" to the security of South Vietnam. The source of this commitment was somewhat ambiguous; according to various Administration spokesmen, the SEATO treaty, the Gulf of Tonkin Resolution, bilateral aid agreements between the United States and South Vietnam, and the determination by the President that such a commitment did in fact exist were all factors.[18]

In passing the National Commitments Resolution, the Senate went on record as asserting that such "commitments" could lawfully exist only as the result of positive affirmations by both the Legislative and Executive branches "by means of a treaty, statute, or concurrent resolution of both Houses of Congress specifically providing for such commitment."[19] The accompanying report further specified that such legislative affirmations should be as specific as possible, should be limited in time and scope, and should explicitly "authorize" or "empower" the President to act, rather than "approve and support the determination of the President" as did the Gulf of Tonkin Resolution.[20]

Both the Johnson and Nixon Administrations opposed the resolution. While Johnson Administration spokesmen suggested that it was unnecessary and unwise, the Nixon Administration went farther, asserting that it might be "inconsistent with the allocation of powers under the Constitution."[21] Such harsh denunciations were symptomatic of the degree to which the Executive branch had come to consider war-making to be its sole prerogative. Equally significant was the fact that the National Commitments Resolution was supported by a number of key conservatives, such as Senators John Stennis (D-MS), Richard Russell (D-GA), and Peter Dominick (R-CO) who had been, and would remain, supporters of U.S. involvement in Southeast Asia. For these men, the issue was not Vietnam but rather the constitutionally mandated separation of powers. In the words of Senator Dominick, "We are almost to the point where Congress is no longer requested to advise on matters of foreign relations, only to consent to what has already been reduced to finality."[22]

The National Commitments Resolution contained the germ of many key ideas that would find their way into the WPR. Most important, the reports on the resolution submitted by the Committee on Foreign Relations in 1967 and 1969 were largely exhaustive examinations of the relative war powers of the Executive and Legislative branches, the issue that Congress had avoided for so long. These reports followed extensive hearings during which legal and constitutional experts, as well as many Members of Congress, testified. The Committee's conclusion put the Senate on record unequivocally regarding its interpretation of the relevant constitutional issues, stating explicitly that the undeniable expansion of Executive war-making power did not constitute a precedent to be followed, but rather an imbalance to be redressed.

> A careful study of the Constitution and of the intent of the framers as set forth in the extensive documentation which they bequeathed to us leaves not the slightest doubt that, except for repelling sudden attacks on the United States, the Founders of our country intended decisions to initiate either general or limited hostilities against foreign countries to be made by the Congress and not by the executive. . . . Only in the present century have Presidents used the armed forces of the United States against foreign governments entirely on their own authority, and only since 1950 have Presidents regarded themselves as having authority to commit the armed forces to full-scale and sustained warfare.[23]

The historic significance of this statement, affirmed by a substantial majority of the Senate, was well understood. In the words of Senate Majority Leader Mike Mansfield (D-MT), "the Senate has acted to reassert its historic and Constitutional role."[24] This assertion, however, took place only at the rhetorical level; the resolution had no force of law. In view of the Executive's continued unwillingness to retreat from precedent, it soon became apparent that more direct action would be needed if the claims of congressional authority set out in 1969 were to be secured.

MOVES AGAINST THE VIETNAM WAR

In the early years of the Nixon Administration, several factors came together to precipitate sweeping new congressional action. The continuation and escalation of the Vietnam War despite Nixon's 1968 pledge to bring it to an end, combined with the rise in public opposition to the war, convinced a number of Members of Congress that the Legislative branch should initiate action to end the war. This belief was further reinforced in April 1970, when President Nixon ordered U.S. troops into Cambodia without informing the Congress in advance, much less consulting with it.

It was symptomatic of the changing mood of Congress and the country that this relatively minor military action generated greater opposition than previous, much more extensive, initiatives. Popular protests against the war, of which the Kent State and Jackson State "massacres" were extreme but not unrepresentative examples, imbued Capitol Hill with a sense of urgency. After almost a decade of tacit (and at times open) acquiescence to the war, Congress would now employ all of the means at its disposal to bring the war to a speedy end.

An initial development of considerable symbolic importance, if little practical consequence, was the 1971 repeal of the Gulf of Tonkin Resolution. Although some congressional leaders (Senators Sam Ervin (D-NC) and Stennis, for example) believed that the repeal ended the President's authority to carry out the war in Southeast Asia, this view did not predominate in Congress and was rejected outright by the Administration. Instead, the Nixon Administration chose to sidestep the dangerous issue of the President's constitutional authority to initiate conflict. Having inherited the Vietnam War from his predecessors, and being publicly committed to bringing it to an end, President Nixon asserted that his responsibility as commander-in-chief to protect the lives of American troops and secure the release of prisoners of war gave him the authority to carry out military policy in Vietnam.[25] Accordingly, the Administration did not oppose repeal of the Tonkin Gulf Resolution.

The Power of the Purse

More significant in the long run were congressional initiatives seeking to legislate an end to the U.S. intervention in Southeast Asia directly. Various legislative vehicles were employed in pursuit of this goal, but a common theme involved using Congress' "power of the purse" to place statutory limits on the President's freedom of action. The authority of Congress to take such action is unquestioned; determining the level and use of federal appropriations is clearly its constitutional prerogative. In practice, though, this strategy often proves difficult to implement and can bring about unintended results. The experience of the early 1970s provided numerous examples of these problems, but it also demonstrated the potential power of such legislation.

During the weeks after the U.S. incursion into Cambodia, Senators George McGovern (D-SD) and Mark Hatfield (R-OR) and Senators John Sherman Cooper (D-KY) and Frank Church (D-ID) introduced amendments that attempted to force an end to specific U.S. military activities in Southeast Asia by withholding the authorization of funds for them. The McGovern-Hatfield Amendment sought to cut off funds for military activity in all of Southeast Asia, setting deadlines for the end of the U.S. presence in Vietnam, Cambodia, and Laos. The Senate defeated the measure by a vote of 55 to 39—a far cry from the 98 to 2 vote in favor of the Gulf of Tonkin Resolution six years before.

The Cooper-Church Amendment was more limited, dealing strictly with Cambodia, and accordingly came closer to success. President Nixon signed into law a modified version, although only after U.S. troops had already been withdrawn from Cambodia. The amendment as signed prohibited the reintroduction of U.S. troops (although not the use of U.S. airpower) into Cambodia and, as such, represented the first presidential acquiescence to a congressionally imposed limit on his war-making powers.[26] The Cooper-Church Amendment was also the focus of a highly publicized month-long debate in the Senate. In addition to examining the merits of the proposed legislation, Senators engaged in the most wide-ranging discussion to date of the President's war powers, thus advancing war powers as a national political issue.

Congress tightened its purse strings again in 1973, after the signing of the Paris peace agreement. When President Nixon, in response to the failure of the Cambodian Communists to observe the cease-fire, resumed bombing operations over Cambodia, Senator Thomas Eagleton (D-MO) sought a means to put a final halt to U.S. military activity in Southeast Asia. Congress' previous refusal to appropriate funds specifically for the bombing operations had been undermined by the military's transfer of spending authority from other programs for this purpose. To circumvent this problem, Eagleton proposed an amendment barring the use of any congressionally appropriated funds for combat operations in Laos or Cambodia.[27] Although it was adopted by a wide margin in the Senate, this amendment met with strong opposition from President Nixon, who vetoed the bill to which it was attached.

The House had originally passed the measure by a close vote of 219 to 188,[28] marking the first time that a majority of the House joined the Senate in open opposition to the war in Indochina. The vote also heralded the growing power of politically motivated junior members, as the Eagleton Amendment was introduced from the floor and passed despite the opposition of much of the House leadership. The margin of victory, however, was well shy of that needed to override a presidential veto. Senate proponents of the bombing cutoff persisted, attaching the measure to successive "must-pass" appropriation and debt-limit bills. In the end, a compromise delayed the end of the bombing for forty-five days but expanded the scope of the limitation to cover all of Southeast Asia—a largely theoretical concession on the part of the Executive since military operations in Vietnam had already ceased.[29]

Certain Members of Congress, notably Senator Eagleton, were dismayed at what they perceived to be a congressional "surrender" in accepting this compromise, which seemed to give congressional sanction—even if only temporarily—to a war they considered illegal.[30] Despite these qualms, the legislation did have its broader desired effects. As of August 15, 1973, all U.S. combat activities in Southeast Asia came to a final halt. The President's acceptance of this measure was at best reluctant, but it was given. House Minority Leader Gerald Ford (R-MI), giving the Administration's view, admitted that "if the President wants to take any military action in Southeast Asia after August 15, he will come to Congress and request that authority."[31]

Problems of Purse-string Legislation

Despite this success, the history of the Eagleton Amendment serves as a clear illustration of the serious limitations inherent in applying purse-string legislation to war powers matters. The Pentagon's ability to shift funds appropriated for one purpose to entirely different uses—in this case, to aerial operations in Cambodia—forced Senator Eagleton and others to resort to very broad legislative language. The sweeping prohibitions that resulted, however, imposed permanent restrictions on U.S. military activities in Southeast Asia, which became problematic in 1975 when the Cambodian and South Vietnamese governments collapsed under renewed Communist attack.

On the international level, the bans on U.S. intervention, as well as the Congress' reluctance to provide large-scale military material assistance to South Vietnam, made the U.S. withdrawal from Southeast Asia seem less like a calculated disengagement than an open rout. The question of the long-term viability of the Saigon regime—certainly a point open to debate—was lost in the general outcry over the U.S. "abandonment" of its allies, a perception that hindered U.S. foreign policy throughout the 1970s. The domestic implications of congressional tactics were also important and persistent. The fact that the final steps in the U.S. pull-out from Vietnam were taken by the Congress allowed Presidents Nixon and Ford to blame the Legislative branch for having "lost" Vietnam. This has become a recurring and effective theme of conservative critics of congressional war powers legislation.[32]

The fate of the Eagleton Amendment also illustrates a problem that may be inherent in purse-string initiatives. In 1973 a majority of Senators wished to end the bombing of Cambodia immediately, whereas the President wanted to retain the option of continuing it indefinitely. Although these positions are diametrically opposed, it is possible to make a case for either on objective military-political grounds. It is difficult, however, to find a logical rationale for the compromise that emerged: the continuation of the bombing for a publicly announced pre-determined period of forty-five days. This action had no demonstrable impact on the eventual outcome of the Cambodian civil war, but it exposed U.S. forces to the hazards of combat for an additional period. The sort of political split-the-difference settlement that may be acceptable in other matters becomes absurd in this context.[33]

In light of the evident shortcomings of purse-string initiatives, one must ask why congressional majorities repeatedly chose these tactics. After 1973 there was an overwhelming desire both in Congress and in the country at large to have nothing further to do with Vietnam, whatever the consequences. In the words of Senator Norris Cotton (R-NH), "As far as I am concerned, I want to get the hell out of there just as quickly as possible, and I don't want to fool around to the point where they might take more prisoners."[34] In pursuit of this end Members of Congress seem to have chosen as they did not so much because these means were particularly desirable but because no alternatives were at hand. Faced with an intransigent Executive, Congress resorted to the only binding authority that could be brought to bear, despite the adverse consequences.

2 THE WAR POWERS RESOLUTION

As congressional opposition to the Vietnam War mounted, a group of Senators and Representatives actively sought a legislative means to increase Congress' influence on military policy. To that end, they reexamined the question of the constitutional separation of powers, intending to put into action the principles that had inspired the National Commitments Resolution of 1969.

This legislative work was carried out slowly and methodically. Both the House Foreign Affairs Committee and the Senate Foreign Relations Committee held extensive hearings on the question of war powers and numerous legislative proposals were considered, modified, and shaped into a final product—the War Powers Resolution of 1973—which represented a broad legislative consensus. The House of Representatives initiated the process.

INITIAL WAR POWERS PROPOSALS

In 1970 a number of measures were introduced in the House that included many of the provisions eventually incorporated into the WPR. Congressman Paul Findley (R-IL), a conservative Republican, introduced an important early proposal (H.R. 18654, 91st Cong.). The key provision of this bill was the requirement that the President submit a detailed report whenever U.S. troops were committed to conflict or introduced into a foreign nation while equipped for combat, even if conflict was not imminent, and when existing U.S. troop deployments abroad were substantially enlarged. These provisions survive in the 1973 WPR.

Congressman Jonathan Bingham (D-NY) suggested a different approach. While Bingham asserted that it was impossible to detail all of the circumstances in which the President might legitimately use the armed forces, his bill (H.R. 18599, 91st Cong.) provided for congressional oversight after the fact by legislating that such presidential initiatives would be automatically terminated if, at any time, either House of Congress passed a resolution of disapproval. Slightly modified as Section 5(c), this is the most controversial provision of the WPR, allowing Congress to terminate a presidentially initiated military operation by a concurrent resolution of both chambers.

The aversion demonstrated by both Findley and Bingham to any explicit description of the specific circumstances in which the President might initiate military action represented the sentiment of the House majority. Whether to include such an enumeration was to become a key controversial issue between House and Senate proponents of war powers.

Sensing a growing consensus in the House, Representative Clement Zablocki (D-WI), chairman of the Subcommittee on National Security Policy and Scientific Developments, before which hearings on the various war powers proposals had been held, offered a legislative proposal of his own. This resolution (H.R. 1355, 91st Cong.), passed by the House on November 16, 1970, centered on a reporting requirement almost identical to Congressman Findley's proposal. In addition, a non-binding provision called for prior consultation between the Congress and the President in emergency situations, another provision that, given full force of law, would appear in the 1973 resolution.

Although Zablocki's resolution was never considered by the Senate, it was the first recognizable version of the WPR passed by at least one House. Moreover, the resolution was not opposed by the Nixon Administration; as such, it can be thought of as defining the limit of oversight the Executive branch would voluntarily accept. Significantly, House opposition to the Zablocki resolution came almost entirely from liberal Democrats, who considered it too weak.

In the Senate, Jacob Javits (R-NY) also introduced a war powers bill in 1970 (S. 3964, 91st Cong.). Javits asserted repeatedly that he did not seek confrontation with the Executive branch but rather wished to fashion an institutional mechanism by which Congress and the President could exercise their collective judgment. Although this language was eventually written into the WPR, key sections of Javits' bill were, from the outset, unacceptable to the Executive. Unlike Representative Findley, Senator Javits believed that it was necessary to enumerate the contingencies in which the President might act unilaterally. A modified version of this enumeration is included in the WPR, although not among the operative clauses.

The Javits bill also contained the first version of what may be considered the most important single provision of the 1973 WPR: the imposition of a finite deadline for any hostilities not approved by Congress. The scenario Javits envisaged was that the President, if he found it necessary to act pursuant to one of the bill's contingencies, would submit a report to Congress similar to that described in the Findley bill, whereupon Congress would have thirty days either to declare war or to provide statutory authorization for the President's action. In the absence of such action, the President's authority to carry out military activities would end. Senator Javits' bill was not considered by the 91st Congress, which chose to focus on addressing the Cooper-Church Amendment and repealing the Gulf of Tonkin Resolution, but the Senate again took up war powers legislation in the 92d Congress.

By 1971 events in Southeast Asia and the Nixon Administration's intransigent attitude had convinced a number of influential Senators that limited measures, such as the Cooper-Church Amendment, and non-binding statements, such as the National Commitments Resolution, were not enough; more sweeping measures were required. Senators Javits and Thomas Eagleton (D-MO) were, as before, at the forefront of this movement, but this time bolstered by the support of Senator John Stennis (D-MS) and a number of conservative Democrats. As a result, only a relatively small group of Senators, mostly conservative Republicans led by

Senator Barry Goldwater (R-AZ), remained steadfast in opposition to any war powers measure. Senator Stennis' active participation, moreover, was of significant consequence to the ultimate shape of the resolution.

The Javits/Eagleton/Stennis bill (S. 2956, 92d Cong.) contained the thirty-day cutoff provision of Javits' earlier proposal, as well as reporting requirements similar to those originally proposed by Congressman Findley. In addition, the bill contained a section that explicitly defined those circumstances in which the President could make "emergency use" of the armed forces in the absence of a declaration of war: (1) to repel armed attack on the United States; (2) to repel armed attack on U.S. military forces abroad (and, in both cases, to forestall direct and imminent threat of such an attack); (3) to protect, while evacuating, U.S. citizens abroad in situations of imminent threat to life; and (4) pursuant to specific statutory authorization.[2]

The bill's opponents based their position on two premises. The first, articulated primarily by Senator Goldwater, was that virtually unlimited war-making power was inherent in the President's position as commander-in-chief, and that numerous precedents supported that claim. Others, such as Senator Gale McGee (D-WY), attacked the bill's practical implications. In the modern world, McGee asserted, it was necessary for the President to retain maximum flexibility to deal with ever changing dangers. McGee, in fact, had raised similar objections to the National Commitments Resolution in 1969, casting the only vote against it in committee and appending a dissenting opinion to the committee's report. The Nixon Administration, for its part, left no doubt that such a bill would be vetoed if it should reach the President's desk. When S. 2956 came up for a final vote, however, its opponents could muster only 16 votes, against 68 in favor.

In the House, a measure virtually identical to Zablocki's 1970 resolution had already been adopted by voice vote. At this point, however, matters reached an impasse, as neither body was willing to compromise its position. Chairman Zablocki and the House remained committed to shaping a bill that would be acceptable to the Executive branch, while the Senate had embarked on a more confrontational path with the inclusion of a strict enumeration of the President's emergency powers and the thirty-day cutoff provision.

PASSAGE OF THE WAR POWERS RESOLUTION

Despite this setback, both Houses again took up war powers measures early in 1973. Following the protracted battle over the Cambodian bombing cutoff, many House backers of war powers legislation, most importantly Chairman Zablocki, had lost any hope and, to a certain extent, desire of finding a solution acceptable to the President, so concentrated instead on achieving agreement with the Senate. At the same time, Javits and other key Senate leaders, eager to get legislation passed, were willing to be more flexible than before.

This greater flexibility, as well as the absolute necessity of retaining the support of Senator Stennis and his conservative colleagues, resulted in a split between Senator Eagleton and the other proponents of war powers legislation. The rift became apparent during the consideration of an amendment proposed by Eagleton that would have made the CIA and other non-military agents of the U.S. Government subject to the bill's provisions. This measure, which was directly inspired by the revelation of the prolonged role that the CIA played in Laos, was supported by Senator William Fulbright (D-AR), the powerful chairman of the Senate Foreign Relations Committee, but it was opposed by Senator Stennis. Knowing the Mississippi Senator's critical importance, Javits and other moderate and liberal backers of war powers legislation refused to support Eagleton in this matter.[3] The resulting bill (S. 440, 93d Cong.), which was nearly identical to the 1972 Senate war powers bill, passed by a vote of 72 to 18—5 more votes than required to overturn a presidential veto.

The House, during this time, passed a war powers measure (H.J.Res. 542, 93d Cong.) that was considerably stronger than Zablocki's bill in the 92d Congress. In particular, it incorporated an automatic cutoff provision similar to that of the Senate bill—although granting the President 120 days rather than 30—and reinstated the provision allowing Congress to terminate a conflict by means of a concurrent resolution of disapproval, which originally had been proposed by Congressman Bingham. By employing this mechanism, Bingham and his allies proposed to avoid the possibility of a presidential veto of resolutions mandating the end of military operations.[4]

It is significant in light of later events that this last measure was opposed by a number of Members, including Chairman Zablocki, who would have preferred to use a joint resolution—requiring the President's signature—for this purpose, as was done in the Senate bill. Proponents of the concurrent resolution found precedents in such past legislation as the Lend-Lease Act, the Emergency Price Control Act, and most recently the Executive Reorganization Act. They also pointed out that both the Middle East and the Tonkin Gulf Resolutions had included provisions making them reversible by concurrent resolution.[5] This would remain one of the most controversial provisions of the WPR.

When the conference committee on war powers legislation was convened, significant differences remained between the House and Senate bills. To the surprise of some participants, however, agreement on most points came relatively easily. The Senate conferees adopted the reporting requirements of the House bill and agreed to the use of a concurrent resolution as the means of ordering termination of military activity. The conferees also reached a compromise on the mandatory cutoff provision by setting the time limit at sixty days, but providing for a nearly automatic extension if the President certified that extra time was necessary to withdraw U.S. forces safely. The most serious point of disagreement proved to be the question of whether to enumerate the President's emergency powers, an issue that the House adamantly refused to consider.

This refusal harkened back to the reluctance of Congress to define presidential war powers in the 1940s and 1950s. House leaders believed that such a provision would weaken the bill. Including a broadly worded enumeration of emergency powers, they argued, risked providing a pretext for an expansion of those powers, as Presidents might seize them as authority for military activities that Congress would wish to prohibit. An overly narrow enumeration, on the other hand, might unduly restrict the President's power to react to sudden international dangers. A better policy, in the minds of the House conferees, was to rely on prior consultation and the possibility of congressionally applied sanctions after the fact.

Senator Eagleton, in particular, disagreed with this position. To him, the definition of the President's power as commander-in-chief was the fundamental purpose of war powers legislation. If it were omitted, the result would be a "dangerous piece of legislation," because it would, in effect, authorize the President to initiate conflict whenever he saw fit and pursue it without sanction for sixty days.[6] The prospect of an automatic cutoff after that period did not comfort Eagleton. As he explained it:

> Congress had been notoriously incapable of stopping a conflict once the flag had been committed. Once a battle is underway, the commander-in-chief controls the flow of vital information; the reins of power, political and military, are in his hands. Under these circumstances, it was unrealistic to expect a majority of Congress to oppose U.S. participation in an ongoing war, especially during the 1st weeks and months of the conflict when the President monopolizes public opinion.[7]

In light of subsequent experience, this statement seems prophetic, although it is not clear that the inclusion of the measures supported by Eagleton would have altered Executive behavior significantly.

The final compromise legislation relegated Eagleton's enumeration clause to the resolution's Purpose and Policy section. Although Javits claimed that this preserved the essence of the Senate position, the conference report on the War Powers Resolution indicates otherwise in its statement that "subsequent sections of this resolution are not dependent on the language of this subsection [2c] as was the case in a similar provision of the Senate bill"; in other words, the subsection was no longer legally binding.[8] Senator Eagleton viewed this wording as evidence of "surrender" and refused to support the resolution as amended.

Joining Eagleton in opposition to the WPR were long-time opponents such as Senators Barry Goldwater and John Tower (R-TX). Speaking in support of the measure in the final Senate debate was an impressive cross-section of the Senate. In addition to Senators Javits and Stennis, Robert Dole (R-KS), Lloyd Bentsen (D-TX), Robert Taft (R-IL), and Claiborne Pell (D-RI) rose in support of the measure. The final vote was 75 to 20, more than enough to override a veto.

In the House, the vote was closer, with opposition coming from both conservative Republican supporters of President Nixon and a group of liberal Democrats who still believed that the bill gave too much power to the President. The final House tally was 238 votes in favor (including 75 by Republicans) and 123 against. Proportionally, this was three votes shy of the two-thirds majority needed to override a veto. A number of Members were absent for the vote, however, and the likelihood of a potential override vote was left unclear.

As expected, President Nixon vetoed the resolution, citing essentially the same objections as had been voiced by Senators Goldwater and McGee. On the theoretical level, Nixon believed that the WPR placed restrictions on "authorities that the President had properly exercised under the Constitution for almost two hundred years." Attempts to limit this authority, in the President's view, were unconstitutional. On the practical level, the WPR "... would seriously undermine the nation's ability to act decisively and convincingly in times of crisis." As a result, Nixon asserted, the confidence of allies would diminish while the respect of adversaries would decline.[9] These arguments were not new, and they appear to have changed few minds in Congress. They are significant, however, as precedent for succeeding Presidents' reservations as to the wisdom and constitutionality of the WPR.[10]

The vote on whether to sustain the President's veto, as is always the case in such situations, was at least partially a vote on the President himself. Reaching the nadir of his popularity due to the growing Watergate scandal, Richard Nixon was in no position to sustain such a test. In the key House vote, eight Republicans who had previously opposed the WPR voted to dissociate themselves from the President, while eight liberal Democrats saw no choice but to oppose him, despite their continued reservations about what they perceived to be a weak and ineffective piece of legislation. These shifts were sufficient; the House joined the Senate in voting to override, and on November 7, 1973, the WPR became law.

PROVISIONS OF THE WAR POWERS RESOLUTION

The text of the WPR as passed in 1973 (P.L. 93-148) was quite brief. It contained ten sections, of which the first and last consisted only of the title and effective date, respectively. (The full text of the WPR is included as an appendix to this book.) Section 2 was entitled Purpose and Policy, distinguishing it as non-binding. In this section, the authors of the WPR sought to define its intent and indicated the constitutional authority on which it was based. Paragraph (c) of Section 2 held the truncated version of the enumeration clause, here denied force of law.

The principal operative provisions of the WPR were in Sections 3 through 5. Section 3 directed the President to consult with Congress before introducing armed forces into hostilities—a binding version of Congressman Zablocki's 1970 proposal. Section 4 spelled out the reporting requirements first proposed by Congressman Findley, directing the President to report to the Congress all non-routine deployments of U.S. armed forces within forty-eight hours of their initiation. Only routine military activities, defined as "deployments which relate solely to supply, replacement, repair, or training" were exempted from this requirement (WPR, Section 4[a]). All reports were to state the circumstances and purposes of the deployment in question, as well as the constitutional or statutory authority under which it was carried out. In cases where U.S. forces were involved in hostilities, further reports were to be made at intervals not to exceed six months, for as long as the situation continued. Section 5(a) specified that all reports submitted under Section 4 should be addressed to the Speaker of the House and the President Pro Tem of the Senate, and provided for these two leaders to call the Congress into special session if it was recessed at the time. The subsequent paragraphs of Section 5 contained the final version of the oversight provisions first introduced by Senator Javits and Congressman Bingham.

Section 5(b) stated that forces committed to actual or imminent hostilities by presidential order must be withdrawn within sixty days unless the Congress declared war, passed legislation specifically authorizing the use of armed force for that particular case, extended the deadline by statute, or was unable to meet following an attack on the United States. The President might unilaterally extend the deadline for thirty days if he certified to the Congress that the additional time was necessary to ensure the safe withdrawal of the forces involved. In addition, Section 5(c) gave Congress authority to direct the President to withdraw U.S. forces at any time, before or after the sixty-day limit, by passing a concurrent resolution to that effect.

Sections 6 and 7 of the WPR set out priority procedures for congressional consideration of legislation introduced pursuant to Sections 5(b) and 5(c). Deadlines were mandated for each step of the legislative process to ensure that final consideration on such legislation would take place within the sixty-day limit imposed by Section 5(b).

Section 8 addressed issues that the resolution's authors considered to require clarification or emphasis. Paragraph (a) specified that no legislation, including security treaties and appropriation acts, would be considered as providing statutory authorization for the introduction of U.S. armed forces into actual or imminent hostilities unless that legislation or treaty specifically authorized such, and stated that Congress intended to do so within the meaning of the WPR. Paragraph (b) qualified this provision by assuring that the WPR was not intended to prevent or require statutory authorization for the participation of U.S. forces in headquarters operations of "high level military commands," such as NATO and NORAD, or in routine joint training exercises with forces of other countries. Paragraph (c), finally, broadly defined the term "introduction of U.S. forces" as including the participation of U.S. troops in operations by foreign forces involved in hostilities, even if U.S. personnel were not themselves exposed to hostilities.

The resolution's final operative statement, contained in Section 9, consisted of a so-called separability clause, which ensured that if any provision of the law were found to be invalid, all other provisions would continue to apply.

CONCLUSION: THE WPR IN PERSPECTIVE

There is no doubt that the political circumstances surrounding the passage of the WPR were extraordinary. The recently terminated Vietnam War had focused attention on questions of war-making authority, while the ongoing Watergate affair put the President in a uniquely weak position. In light of the lengthy legislative history of the WPR, however, it is not only incorrect but disingenuous to characterize it as a spur-of-the-moment act of legislative reprisal against an unpopular President. While opposition to President Nixon undeniably helped turn around key votes in 1973, the genesis of the WPR lay in the late 1960s.

The 91st and 92d Congresses had set important precedents by using their fiscal power to impose limits on Executive war-making. Legislation such as the Cooper-Church and Eagleton Amendments demonstrated that ongoing military operations could be halted by congressional action. At the same time, however, these measures illustrated that such congressional "victories" can carry a heavy political and diplomatic cost. Rather than providing a desirable model for future Legislative-Executive relations, the purse-string measures highlighted the necessity for a more permanent framework acceptable to both branches, through which Congress could participate directly in the decision to commit military forces from the outset. Without such a framework, the risk of institutional paralysis was dangerously real.

In this context, the WPR was the legislative result of a concerted effort on the part of congressional leaders to provide such a framework. Through it, they hoped to regain a measure of constructive influence in foreign policy by asserting the constitutional powers of the Congress to participate in decision-making with respect to the deployment and commitment of armed forces. The resolution begins with a clear statement to this effect:

> The Purpose of this Joint Resolution is to fulfill the intent of the framers of the Constitution of the United States of America and ensure that the collective judgment of both the Congress and the President will apply to the introduction of United States armed forces into hostilities or situations where imminent involvement in hostilities is clearly indicated by the circumstances, and to the continued use of such forces in hostilities or in such situations. [WPR, Section 2(a)]

In practical terms, congressional proponents of war powers legislation sought to ensure that Congress would never again be presented with a fait accompli, such as President Truman's intervention into Korea, or allow itself to relinquish its constitutional prerogatives (intentionally or otherwise), as they concluded had happened with the passage of the Gulf of Tonkin Resolution and its predecessors. In the words of Senator Stennis:

> ... We must ensure that this country never again goes to war without the moral sanction of the American people. This is important both in principle and as practical politics. Vietnam has shown us that in trying to fight a war without the clear-cut prior support of the American people we not only risk military ineffectiveness but we also strain the very structure of the Republic.[11]

3 REVOLUTION OR LOST OPPORTUNITIES?

While passage of the War Powers Resolution over President Nixon's veto represented a clear victory for the Congress in the near term, the longer run triumph of the congressional position on the broad issue of war powers was by no means assured. Executive opposition to the idea of a renewed assertion of congressional war powers did not end with the override of President Nixon's veto. Instead, Nixon's successors consistently expressed reservations concerning both the wisdom and the constitutionality of the WPR.

The early record of the resolution's implementation and the initial precedents established for key sections of the WPR, as well as the continuing debate on the more general problem of the resolution's constitutionality, are telling. A close look at the relative success of the reporting, consultation, and oversight provisions will build a better understanding of the limits and potential demonstrated in the first years of the WPR's existence.

On a superficial level, the legislation was successfully implemented; the Executive branch attempted neither to pursue an immediate legal challenge nor to ignore the new law entirely. The Ford and Carter Administrations invoked the WPR on several occasions, submitting to Congress a total of five reports on:[1]

1. Danang sealift (1975)—evacuation of U.S. and Vietnamese refugees
2. Cambodian evacuation (1975)—evacuation of U.S. personnel from Phnom Penh
3. Saigon evacuation (1975)—evacuation of U.S. and Vietnamese personnel from Vietnam
4. *Mayaguez* incident (1975)—rescue of the crew of the U.S. freighter *Mayaguez* from Cambodian forces
5. Iran rescue (1980)—attempted rescue of U.S. hostages in Tehran

In each of these cases, however, questions were raised by Members of Congress and other observers as to whether the new law had been complied with fully. Moreover, questions arose in several other cases in which the WPR might arguably have been invoked but was not. The most controversial of these involved reconnaissance flights over Cambodia in 1975, the so-called tree-cutting incident in the Korean Demilitarized Zone in 1976, and the airlift of French and Belgian troops to Zaire by U.S. aircraft in 1978.[2]

Despite these questions of implementation and a number of other lingering problems and debates, the Congress proved unwilling, during the Ford and Carter Administrations, to pursue the issue of full implementation aggressively, or to clarify ambiguities in the resolution's language. The net result of this process was not, as some had predicted, the reduction of the WPR to a purely symbolic position. By 1980, however, it was clear that the WPR would play a different role than that intended by its authors. Rather than being a set of specific procedures, the WPR came to represent a broad, but nonetheless significant, definition of both the extent of and the limits to the Executive's effective freedom of action with respect to the employment of U.S. armed forces.

PROBLEMS OF SCOPE AND CONSTITUTIONALITY

The legal and theoretical debate over the WPR continued after the law's passage, focusing on two issues. Uncertainty over the scope and intent of the WPR, and in particular the significance of the enumeration clause in Section 2, had the unfortunate effect of confusing the general debate and obscuring more relevant issues. In addition, the resolution's constitutionality was questioned by the Executive branch, as well as by certain legal and academic observers.

The Enumeration of Presidential Powers

Section 2(c) of the WPR specifies that the President's power as commander-in-chief to introduce troops into hostilities is applicable (1) following a declaration of war, (2) pursuant to other specific statutory authorization, and (3) in response to a national emergency created by an attack on U.S. territories or armed forces. The language of this section seems definite when it states that "the constitutional powers of the President as commander-in-chief . . . *are exercised only pursuant to. . . .*" (emphasis added) The 1973 House-Senate Conference deliberately placed this statement in the Purpose and Policy section, however, to segregate it from the operative clauses that follow. Despite its seemingly prescriptive language, this statement was understood by the conferees as defining a minimum congressional consensus on the extent of the President's war powers, rather than as an exhaustive and legally binding enumeration of specific authority.

The ambiguity of Section 2(c) made it one of the most problematic sections in the years immediately following the resolution's passage. A particularly troublesome point was the question of the President's authority to use the armed forces to rescue U.S. citizens abroad. All five cases in which formal reports under the WPR were filed by Presidents Ford and Carter included such rescues in one way or another. The President's authority to carry out these operations was never seriously questioned in Congress, even though the rescue of citizens abroad is not found among the instances listed in Section 2(c).

The omission of citizen rescue missions as a legitimate basis for the President to employ troops abroad was the deliberate result of House Members' concern that such authority, if stated explicitly, would be open to abuse by Presidents who would conduct broad military initiatives under the guise of rescue operations. In practice, the President's authority to carry out "legitimate" rescue missions was reaffirmed repeatedly. Section 2(c) was thus demonstrated to be nonexclusive; Congress recognized the fact that the President might properly exercise his power as commander-in-chief pursuant to developments other than those cited there, subject to the sanctions contained in the remaining provisions of the WPR. Senator Eagleton and others made several attempts to restore force of law to the WPR's enumeration of the President's powers, but they were thwarted by the persistence of the political forces that had forced the 1973 compromise.

Despite these illustrations of congressional intent, the seemingly prescriptive language of Section 2(c) made it a favorite target of those who argued that the WPR put undue restrictions on the President. While these arguments were not borne out in practice, they contributed to lingering doubts concerning the viability of the WPR as a whole. More regrettably, the debate over Section 2(c) clouded objective analysis of the resolution's desirability and effectiveness by making it seem much broader in intent than its framers had agreed that it would be.

Constitutional Authority

Of much greater significance than the debate over the enumeration of powers were the questions raised concerning the constitutionality of the operative sections of the WPR, particularly the oversight provisions of Section 5.

The authors of the WPR, believing that twentieth-century Presidents had overstepped the bounds of their constitutional war-making authority, had intended to reassert a more proper balance of power and, in so doing, overturn recently established precedents. In particular, they held that while the President might, in certain cases, commit armed forces on his own authority, the decision to maintain them in hostile situations must always be made by the Congress. This position was based on a particular interpretation of the Constitution, and on certain precedents drawn from the early history of the Republic; its political force came from the conclusion that excessive executive power had led directly to serious policy errors that might otherwise have been avoided.

Congressional proponents of the WPR were well aware, however, that this view was not shared by the Executive branch. Accordingly, they sought to provide an explicit statement of constitutional authority within the resolution's text. To this end, Section 2(b) invokes the so-called necessary and proper clause of the Constitution, which empowers the Congress to make laws "necessary and proper for carrying into execution not only its own powers but also all other powers vested by the Constitution in the Government of the United States, or in any department or officer thereof. . . ." (WPR, Section 2[b]) While the text of the resolution does not elaborate, the context of the legislation makes it clear that, in this case, the Congress proposed to regulate the exercise of the President's power as commander-in-chief by establishing procedures to be followed whenever he acts in that capacity. Since broad agreement already existed as to the proper exercise of this power following a congressional declaration of war, most of the resolution's operative provisions cover situations in which war has not been formally declared.

The question of constitutional authority is also addressed in Section 8(d), which states that the WPR is not intended to invalidate existing treaties or to alter the constitutional powers of either the Congress or the President. On one level, the latter statement is self-evident. No statute, short of a constitutional amendment, can alter the constitutional authority of a branch of the federal government. As we have seen, however, considerable disagreement existed prior to the passage of the WPR as to the actual relative constitutional powers of the Executive and Legislative branches. With the passage of the WPR, Congress put forward its interpretation of what the balance of power should be.

The imprecision of the Constitution on this point is such that those believing that the President's war powers are effectively limitless could also base their case on an interpretation of constitutional provisions. In addition they could point to an extensive body of recent precedents. For those holding this view, the WPR was not a return to constitutional principles but an unwise—indeed unlawful—attempt to alter them. Presidents Nixon and Ford held this view explicitly; President Carter's actions suggest that he was at least influenced by it.

At the heart of the debate on constitutionality were the provisions of Section 5 that terminated the President's unilateral authority to maintain

U.S. forces in hostilities after sixty days or following a concurrent resolution of disapproval. These assertions of congressional power stood in direct contradiction to those of virtually unbounded prerogative claimed by Presidents since 1950.

The Ford Administration's position on this matter came across clearly in the testimony of the State Department's legal advisor Monroe Leigh before the House Foreign Affairs Committee following the *Mayaguez* incident, which included the following exchange between Leigh and Representative Stephen Solarz (D-NY):

> *Mr. Solarz*: If the President has sent the troops in pursuant to his constitutional authority, the War Powers Resolution can't require him to withdraw the troops after 90 days. Is that your position?
>
> *Mr. Leigh*: Yes, I agree with that.[3]

Leigh went on to suggest similar objections to those provisions of the WPR that allow Congress to terminate hostilities by means of a concurrent resolution. For Leigh, the key to both of these questions was the fact that the WPR does not represent a congressional delegation of power to the President, since that power did not belong to the Congress in the first place.

> This resolution does not delegate anything to the President.... Therefore, the argument that this is like some of the earlier examples where Congress created a concurrent resolution procedure to control the exercise of authority delegated to the President... is arguable. There is nothing delegated here.[4]

Since the actual events that sparked this exchange did not force a direct confrontation (U.S. forces were not in hostile situations for anywhere near sixty days, and Congress did not attempt to force their withdrawal by means of a concurrent resolution), this conflict of constitutional interpretation between the two branches remained unresolved. The significance of these theoretical reservations, however, was not lost on Congressman Solarz.

> I suppose one can't manufacture legal tests, but I think that we are in a very anomalous situation here in the Congress. We operate on the assumption that we have written a bill which very thoughtfully deals with these problems, which attempts the establishment of restrictions on the use of American forces abroad without a congressional declaration of war, and then the spokesman for the administration tells us that the very limitations contained in the War

Powers Resolution are themselves an unconstitutional restraint on the authority of the President.[5]

The Carter Administration was more circumspect, but in the end, no more forthcoming. In testimony before the Senate Foreign Relations Committee, Herbert Hansell, the State Department's legal advisor for the Carter Administration, stated that the Administration did not intend to challenge the constitutionality of any portion of the WPR. He refused, however, to affirm that the Administration considered the entire WPR to be fully and unambiguously constitutional.[6]

THE EARLY RECORD OF IMPLEMENTATION

The latent but unresolved disagreement over the constitutionality of the WPR underscored, and to a large extent defined, the debates over specific provisions and events that took place from 1974 to 1980. These, in turn, did much to define the practical impact that the WPR would have on the future conduct of U.S. foreign policy. By examining the relative success with which the various sections of the new law were implemented, we can assess the goals and methods of the many participants of this complex debate.

The operative provisions of the WPR direct the President to report to Congress all non-routine deployments of armed forces and to consult with Congress prior to committing armed forces to hostile situations. In its most far-reaching, and most controversial, provision, the WPR establishes a mechanism for congressional oversight of the employment of U.S. armed forces in situations of actual or imminent hostilities. In the years immediately following passage of the WPR, these measures were implemented with varying degrees of success.

Prompt Reporting

The WPR divides military activities that must be reported to Congress into three categories. The first, covered in Section 4(a)(1), is the introduction of forces into "hostilities or situations where imminent involvement in hostilities is clearly indicated by circumstances" (hereafter referred to as 'actual or imminent hostilities'). This section was cited only once, by President Ford in his report on the *Mayaguez* incident. Section 4(a)(2) requires a report if troops armed for combat are introduced into situations where hostilities are not considered imminent. President Ford cited this section in his 1975 reports on the Danang sealift and the Phnom Penh evacuation. Finally, Section 4(a)(3) requires that a report be submitted when the U.S. military presence in any foreign country is "substantially enlarged." This section was never cited by Ford or Carter.

The distinction among these three categories is of considerable significance: the introduction of troops into actual or imminent hostilities, covered in Section 4(a)(1), triggers other provisions of the resolution, in particular the sixty-day limit in Section 5, while the other two require no presidential action beyond reporting. Presidents Carter and Ford endeavored to avoid this distinction by omitting reference to any particular section of the WPR when submitting their reports on the Saigon airlift and the Iran hostage rescue attempt, leaving Congress with the onus of determining under which section of the WPR a given report should be considered.

This practice was challenged in the first hearing to review compliance with the WPR, following the evacuations from Danang, Phnom Penh, and Saigon in 1975. At that time, Monroe Leigh, the State Department's legal advisor, explained that as the President was uncertain at the outset whether hostilities would result from the Saigon operation, he could not cite a specific subsection in his report. Leigh then went on to make the seemingly contradictory claim that the brevity of the operation was such that it was over by the time the report covering it was submitted, rendering moot the question of the sixty-day limit, and thus the need to cite particular subsections. While several Members, including Senator Jacob Javits (R-NY), expressed doubts as to the validity of this reasoning, the matter was dropped with no attempt to prescribe guidelines for future citation of Section 4 in executive reports.[7]

In addition, Section 4 has proven to contain a number of definitional problems. The most serious of these is the lack of a definition for the term *hostilities* in Section 4(a)(1). Since it is precisely the state of actual or imminent hostilities that distinguishes Section 4(a)(1), which triggers the oversight provisions of Section 5, from Section 4(a)(2), which does not, the point is crucial. The 1973 House report on its war powers bill indicates the intent of the legislation's drafters, noting that "the word hostilities was substituted for the phrase armed conflict . . . because it was considered to be somewhat broader in scope. In addition to a situation in which fighting actually has begun, hostilities also encompass a state of confrontation in which no shots have been fired, but in which there is a clear and present danger of armed conflict."[8] This statement, however, does not have force of law, and there is no indication that it has ever been accepted by the Executive branch.

Indeed, one of the few formal exchanges between Congress and the Executive concerning this definitional problem exposed the two branches' interpretational differences rather than defining a consensus. In response to a question put to him by Congressman Clement Zablocki (D-WI) in 1975, Monroe Leigh gave the Ford Administration's working definition: "Hostilities was used to mean a situation in which units of the U.S. armed forces were actively engaged in exchanges of fire with opposing units of hostile forces."[9] While leading congressional proponents of the WPR noted and criticized the disparity, little progress was made in resolving this critical issue.

A second potential ambiguity follows from the fact that Sections 4(a)(2) and 4(a)(3) refer to troops "equipped for combat." It soon became clear that this language would exclude unarmed forces from the scope of the WPR, even if they were employed for overtly military missions. When President Ford asserted the resolution's nonapplicability to unarmed reconnaissance flights over Cambodia in 1975, the Administration's interpretation was generally accepted despite some Members' reservations as to the necessity for and wisdom of the flights themselves.

A more ambiguous case arose in 1978, when President Carter used U.S. military aircraft to airlift French and Belgian troops to Zaire, where an insurgency was in progress. In response to questions posed by Congressman Paul Findley (R-IL) and others, the Carter Administration cited the fact that U.S. personnel were unarmed—although their aircraft carried military equipment and foreign combat troops—as the chief reason why the WPR did not apply in this case. Findley did not accept this argument and requested that hearings be held on the issue. Zablocki's Foreign

Affairs Committee did hold such a hearing, but there proved to be little support for confrontation with the Administration on this relatively minor aspect of a largely noncontroversial action, and the question was not pursued.[10]

Finally, there is a potential problem in Section 4(a)(3) with the undefined term *substantial increase*. As with *hostilities*, a definition for this term does exist in the 1973 House Report on War Powers. In that document, the definition is intentionally broad, noting the need for flexibility in interpretation, but it does suggest guidelines. Sending 1,000 additional troops to Europe, the report suggests, would not be significant, whereas deploying the same number to Guantanamo Bay would be. Interestingly, the one historical example cited, President Kennedy's 1962 decision to increase the number of U.S. advisors in South Vietnam from 700 to 16,000, the report asserts, would have fallen under Section 4(a)(3) had the WPR existed at the time.[11] While this section has yet to be cited by either Congress or the President, experience with other potentially ambiguous sections suggests that an Executive wishing to avoid the reporting requirement could exploit this problem to do so.

Indeed, the exchange of views that took place on the only occasion when implementation of Section 4(a)(3) was considered does not set a hopeful precedent. Following the so-called tree-cutting incident in the Korean Demilitarized Zone in 1976, President Ford reinforced U.S. troops in Korea. This involved, among other moves, deploying of several squadrons of tactical aircraft. In response to congressional questions regarding the applicability of Section 4(a)(3) to this action, the State Department's acting legal advisor agreed that the addition of the aircraft was militarily significant but pointed out that the language of the WPR refers only to number of personnel, not to the military potential of equipment.[12] It is a fact that neither Section 2(a)(3) nor the guidelines in the House Report explicitly disallow this interpretation. Once again, however, the Executive was allowed the narrowest possible reading of a provision limiting presidential freedom of action.

In an ideal atmosphere of Legislative-Executive cooperation, these definitional ambiguities would not present serious problems; generally accepted common-sense definitions of the various terms would prevail. In such an ideal world, however, the WPR itself, which is essentially nothing more than an attempt to clarify an ambiguous aspect of the Constitution, would have been unnecessary. Given the prevailing adversarial atmosphere between recent Presidents and the Congress concerning war powers issues, the ambiguities and undefined terms of Section 4 have given successive Presidents the means to circumvent the WPR entirely, or at least to avoid its more restrictive sections, without provoking an all-out constitutional clash with the Congress.

Prior Consultation

Section 3 of the WPR states that the President shall "in every possible instance" consult with Congress before introducing U.S. armed forces into situations of actual or imminent hostilities. As with Section 4, successive Presidents have taken advantage of ambiguities in this section to retain the greatest possible freedom of action.

President Ford maintained that directing a subordinate to inform congressional leaders—in the *Mayaguez* incident, *after* the start of military operations—fulfilled his responsibility under Section 3.[13] In general, the Executive branch seems to have interpreted "consult" to mean "inform" rather than "seek the advice of." This is not what the House of Representatives had in mind when the consulting requirement was conceived, as is clearly shown in the 1973 committee report on the WPR.

> A considerable amount of attention was given to the definition of "consultation." *Rejected was the notion that consultation should be synonymous with merely being informed.* Rather, consultation in this provision means that a decision is pending on a problem and that Members of Congress are being asked by the President for their advice and opinions and, in appropriate circumstances, their approval of actions contemplated. Furthermore, in order for consultation to be meaningful, *the President himself has to participate* and all information relevant to the situation must be made available. (emphasis added)[14]

Congressional leaders repeatedly criticized the Executive's failure to live up to the spirit of this provision, but no concrete steps were taken to clarify its language.

A second phrase that Presidents Ford and Carter used to advantage was the qualification that the Congress be consulted "in every possible instance." Ford argued that the urgency of the situation made prior consultation impossible in the *Mayaguez* incident, while Carter cited security considerations as reasons for entirely avoiding prior consultation in the attempted Iranian hostage rescue.

In the Senate hearings that followed the Iranian operation, Acting Secretary of State Warren Christopher, while denying that the Carter Administration intended to set a precedent by its actions, admitted implicitly that it considered any consultation with Congress incompatible with secrecy. Had the mission gone as planned, Christopher explained, Congress would have been consulted "at a time so late that the compromise of secrecy would not have been as great."[15] This statement induced angry reactions from Senators who pointed out that consultation with a select group of congressional leaders was no more a breach of secrecy than was the necessary involvement of numerous Executive branch and military personnel, but again no concrete steps were taken to give legislative force to these objections.

These incidents point to a further weakness in Section 3, the fact that the WPR fails to establish a mechanism for consultation. While it is clearly not feasible for all Members of Congress to be consulted prior to urgent and sensitive military operations, the law does not state which Members should be. A 1970 attempt by Representative Zablocki and others to establish a Joint Committee on National Security as a companion measure to war powers legislation had encountered stiff opposition in the House Rules Committee and was never considered by the full House. Even so, common sense would indicate that the appropriate Members should include the leadership of each House, and perhaps of relevant committees. It is from this group that President Ford chose the Members to be informed on the occasion of the Southeast Asia evacuations and the *Mayaguez* incident. The impossibility of consulting all Members continues to provide a ready pretext for avoiding consultation altogether. It has certainly been an effective debating point for academic opponents of the WPR.

One unsuccessful attempt to address the weakness of Section 3 was made by Representative John Seiberling (D-OH) in the wake of the *Mayaguez* incident. Seiberling proposed an amendment to Section 3 substituting the words "seek the advice and council of Congress" for "consult with Congress." The Seiberling amendment further required that the Members so consulted should include, although need not be limited to, a specified group of congressional leaders, and that consultation should occur before a final decision on the introduction of U.S. forces is made.[16] Chairman Zablocki agreed at the time that it was not his intent, in writing Section 3, to require the President to consult with every Member of Congress, but once again there proved to be little interest in defining by statute the particular Members who would be consulted.[17] A similar effort by Senator Eagleton met with the same fate. In general, the vested interests embodied in the existing committee structure of both Houses scuttled the designation of a predetermined body of Members to be responsible for initial consultation with the President on war powers questions.

It is notable that although he was less than enthusiastic about the WPR's consultation provision, President Ford at least claimed to be abiding by it. Since consultation is required only in cases involving actual or imminent hostilities (i.e., the precise conditions referred to in Section 4(a)(1)), such consultation could be taken as implicit presidential acceptance that the situation in question fits the criteria set out in Section 4(a)(1)—whether or not that section was actually cited in the President's subsequent report—and that the oversight provisions triggered by the section would be operative accordingly. There is some evidence to indicate that the Ford Administration anticipated this argument: speaking for the Administration, Monroe Leigh stressed that the President had elected to consult, but was not legally required to do, in the cases in question (the evacuations from Danang, Phnom Penh, and Saigon).[18]

Congressional Oversight of Military Operations

Section 5(b), the so-called sixty-day clock, was intended by the WPR's authors to be the law's central feature, but in practice it proved difficult to test. This was due both to the nature of U.S. military operations in the 1970s and to the Executive hedging noted above. In particular, implementation of Section 5(b) was hindered by the fact that it makes specific reference to reports submitted under Section 4(a)(1). By avoiding reference to any particular section of the WPR in their reports on the Saigon airlift and the Iranian rescue attempt, Presidents Ford and Carter created the possibility that Congress may have to determine whether Section 5(b) applies in any given case.

In fact, Section 5(b) implicitly provides for such a congressional initiative, stating that the use of U.S. armed forces shall be terminated "within 60 days after a report is submitted *or is required to be submitted* pursuant to Section 4(a)(1)." (emphasis added) Practically, however, making such a determination has been extremely difficult for the Congress; every President since the enactment of the WPR has resisted the idea that his powers as commander-in-chief can be limited by statute. Accordingly, Members of Congress who attempted to trigger the clock provision have automatically been put into the position of opposing the President and at least appearing to oppose the military operation in question—an unenviable position if presidentially initiated action enjoyed broad popular support. In such cases, it seems likely that whatever congressional desire might exist to implement fully the operational sections of the WPR would be overwhelmed by the political imperatives of the situation.

The brevity of U.S. military operations in the 1970s precluded a full test of Section 5(b) during the Ford and Carter Administrations. No operation in those years involved U.S. troops in actual or imminent hostilities for longer than sixty days. Thus the Executive branch could pursue a policy of nonrecognition toward the section, refusing to admit that the President as commander-in-chief would ultimately be bound by it, while at the same time avoiding the constitutional confrontation that could ensue if the WPR were flouted openly.

Additional Definitions and Clarifications

A final source of controversy was the extremely broad definition of the "introduction of U.S. armed forces" provided in Section 8(c), which includes the assignment of U.S. troops to "command, coordinate, participate in the movement of, or accompany the regular or irregular military forces of any foreign country or government when such military forces are engaged, or there exists an imminent threat that such forces will be engaged, in hostilities."

The 1973 Senate report's explanation makes it clear that this subsection was included "to prevent a repetition of many of the most controversial and regrettable actions in Indochina," in particular the ever growing role of U.S. advisors in Vietnam and Laos.[19] Section 8(c) could be interpreted even more broadly, however. The implication of this provision is that the U.S. forces themselves need not be exposed to hostilities in order for the WPR to apply to their activities, so long as they are involved with foreign troops who are so exposed.

Congressman Paul Findley (R-IL) cited this interpretation of Section 8(c) as part of his assertion that the Zaire airlift fell under the provisions of the WPR. Not surprisingly, the Carter Administration did not share his opinion, claiming instead that U.S. aircraft had deposited foreign troops far from the scene of actual fighting, and thus did not accompany them or participate in their movements.[20] As noted above, Findley's arguments on the Zaire issue failed to convince the majority of his colleagues, and the matter was not pursued. Still, Section 8(c) offers a potentially powerful method for preventing—or at least affording a measure of congressional control over—the kind of creeping involvement by military advisors that preceded the large-scale employment of U.S. combat troops in Southeast Asia.

MOTIVES AND STRATEGIES

Looking beyond the details of language and specific implementation debates, it is possible to discern broader trends in the behavior of the Executive and Legislative branches during the 1970s. During these years, the Executive branch seemed to develop a coherent and largely effective strategy for dealing with the WPR. The success of the Administrations' efforts, in turn, highlighted certain practical limitations on congressional behavior. At the same time, the trends and patterns apparent during this period left little doubt that the WPR, for all of its imperfections, did have an impact on the institutional balance of power, and on the framework for U.S. foreign policymaking.

Executive Branch Strategy

Taken to its logical extreme, Executive opposition to the WPR could have led to constitutional confrontation. As we have seen, however, Presidents Ford and Carter chose a more subtle approach. Rather than provoking a direct confrontation with the Congress, they dealt with the resolution on a case-by-case basis, never overtly challenging it. By taking advantage of semantic ambiguities and exploiting political situations, Ford and Carter largely reshaped the practical effects of the WPR.

Facilitating this strategy was the fact that the resolution's major provisions—for reporting, consultation, and oversight—were not equally problematic. Executive reactions to the various legislative proposals that went into the making of the 1973 WPR provide considerable insight into these differences.

As early as 1970, when the Nixon Administration gave tacit approval to Congressman Findley's original war powers proposal, the Executive branch signaled that it would be willing, at least in principle, to accept a reporting provision. Statements made by Nixon Administration spokesmen at the time of the final conference on the WPR, while sharply critical of the House and Senate bills in general, welcomed the reporting provisions of both bills as a positive development. When the Nixon and Ford Administrations were presented with repeated queries from the chairmen of the House Foreign Affairs and Senate Foreign Relations Committees as to how the State and Defense Departments intended to comply with the WPR, their official response dealt exclusively with the procedure by which the departments proposed to comply with the reporting requirement. No mention was made of consultation, much less of oversight.[21]

The Executive's position on consultation was less straightforward. Throughout the period in which war powers legislation was being shaped in the Congress, Administration spokesmen claimed that the President understood the importance of cooperating with the Legislative branch and would welcome opportunities for meaningful consultation. Such statements always included reservations, however. In an "emergency" the President must act quickly and consequently would be forced to act alone. Thus, Nixon could accept Zablocki's 1970 war powers bill, which suggested, but did not require, consultation with Congress before armed forces were committed to hostilities. As we have seen, the Ford and Carter Administrations were able to exploit the language of Section 3 of the WPR, as well as imposing their own definitions of "consult," to reduce the scope of the WPR's consultation requirement to a level that President Nixon would have been willing to accept.

The strong negative response to the various war powers measures introduced by Senator Javits and Congressman Bingham underscored the Executive branch's fierce opposition to institutionalized congressional oversight of military activities. The notion that the President's authority to maintain troops in combat might be terminated, or could expire automatically at the end of a predetermined period, was rejected as unconstitutional by the Nixon and Ford Administrations and was never accepted overtly by President Carter.

It is not surprising to find a pattern emerging from the practice of selective compliance established by Presidents Ford and Carter. At least implicitly, the Executive branch chose to comply not with the WPR of 1973 but rather with Zablocki's 1970 bill, which required reporting, suggested consultation, and made no mention whatsoever of oversight. In so doing, the Executive succeeded in avoiding effective congressional challenges, while retaining maximum presidential freedom of action and, even more important, reserving the position that the WPR as a whole might not be ultimately binding.

The language in all of Presidents Ford and Carter's WPR reports subtly but effectively reinforced this position. In each case, the President emphasized that the action in question was taken pursuant to his authority as commander-in-chief, while references to the WPR were worded so as to imply that Executive compliance with the resolution might be voluntary. President Ford "took note of" various subsections while Carter admitted only to submitting a report "consistent with the reporting provisions" of the WPR. By failing to take effective action against it, Congress allowed the position that the WPR was less than fully binding to survive and gain strength. It seems fair to conclude that, by the end of the 1970s, the precedents accumulated by the Ford and Carter Administrations had established this interpretation as the Executive branch's official position on the WPR.

In addition, Presidents and their spokesmen attempted overtly (in the case of President Ford) or implicitly (in that of President Carter) to discredit the WPR by pointing to the excessive restraints that, they claimed, it placed on the President's authority and flexibility. In addition, they emphasized the resolution's inconsistencies and the potential problems that might result from its strict implementation.

In an unfortunate, although perhaps inevitable development, both Presidents Ford and Carter (to say nothing of academic opponents of the WPR) exaggerated the resolution's scope and intentions in their public statements so as to bolster their case against it. President Carter, for example, claimed that his decision to send only a squadron of unarmed F-15s to the Persian Gulf during the Iranian revolution was necessitated by the WPR, a position that seems at best difficult to justify on the basis of the resolution's actual provisions.[22] President Ford, for his part, was fond of pointing out the sometimes comical difficulties involved in consulting Members of Congress on very short notice, conveniently ignoring the fact that this sort of last-minute pro forma consultation was precisely one of the practices that the Resolution's authors had hoped to eliminate.[23]

In their rhetoric, opponents of the WPR tended to equate the resolution's consulting and reporting requirements with outright prohibitions on presidential action; yet in practice, Presidents interpreted the provisions as loosely as possible. This double standard did little to encourage an objective assessment of the resolution's merits and flaws.

Congressional Restraint

Statements made by Members of Congress who followed these matters closely indicate clearly that they were aware of the implications of Executive hedging. The obvious question to consider is why Congress did not do more to impose its own views on Presidents who, relative to their immediate predecessors, were quite weak politically.

In part, the answer seems to lie in the fact that the WPR's language was, as we have seen, the product of lengthy and difficult congressional negotiations. The final resolution represented not so much a synthesis as cumulation of different ideas couched in carefully drafted compromise language. Needing to gather enough votes to override a near certain presidential veto, proponents of the WPR were forced to fashion a piece of legislation that included provisions appealing to as many as possible of the diverse groups and individuals who had expressed support for any portion of the general idea of congressional war powers legislation while, at the same time, avoiding language or provisions unacceptable to any key Member. Given these limitations, the WPR was a remarkable compromise. Nevertheless, the legacy of its origin created a number of practical problems for its implementation.

In seeking to present an unobjectionable bill, the authors of the WPR not only omitted certain highly controversial measures, such as the binding enumeration of presidential powers and all reference to covert military operations, but left in many ambiguities and undefined terms. Their tactic was successful in obtaining the votes necessary for passage. It allowed various Members to interpret the resolution in such a way as to be able to support it. In subsequent years, however, imprecision of several key provisions proved to be a significant weakness for the WPR as a whole, while the risk of unraveling the intricate network of compromises that had gone into its drafting made the resolution effectively impossible to amend.

Likewise, in order to ensure its broad appeal, the resolution as passed included aspects of most of the war powers proposals introduced since the late 1960s. This did not weaken the bill directly, as the various provisions tended to be complementary, but it did portend future problems in enforcing specific sections of the legislation—particularly the consultation and oversight provisions. Members who had voted in favor of the resolution, but who had an abiding personal interest in only one or two of its provisions, proved unwilling to take political risks to defend other aspects of the WPR.

Moreover, certain Members of Congress, although they had voted for the WPR, seemed to harbor lingering doubts as to its wisdom and even its constitutionality. Some of these doubts were voiced in the 1977 Senate War Powers hearings. At that time, Senator John Sparkman (D-AL), who had succeeded Fulbright as chairman of the Senate Foreign Relations Committee, saw fit to remind the committee repeatedly that doubts as to the constitutionality of the WPR had been expressed by Senator John Sherman Cooper (D-KY), a respected constitutional expert, when the Resolution was originally debated and that, in the absence of a definitive judicial test, the question was still open.[24] Over the course of the same hearings, Senators Frank Church (D-ID) and Clifford Case (R-NJ), who were the committee's senior members and had voted for the WPR in

1973, expressed reservations concerning the workability of the resolution's consultation provisions remarkably similar to those voiced by President Ford.[25] While these men never seriously considered repealing the WPR, the doubts they expressed help to explain Congress' unwillingness to consider amendments to strengthen or even clarify particular sections of the WPR, and may be part of the reason why the Congress was not more active in challenging Executive compliance practices.

Conclusion

If one looked solely at the question of implementing the WPR, it would be easy to conclude that the period from the passage of the WPR in 1973 through the end of the Carter Administration in 1980 was marked chiefly by lost opportunities on the congressional side and lack of goodwill on the part of successive Presidents.

The ambiguous record of presidential compliance seems particularly unfortunate in view of the fact that none of President Ford's or Carter's military operations would have been materially affected in any way if these Presidents had chosen to follow a policy of full and unambiguous compliance with the WPR. None of the actions in question were particularly controversial with regard to their desirability, nor did any involve commitments of troops for more than sixty days. Prior consultation and unambiguous reporting would have cost these Presidents no freedom of action.

In general, the evidence suggests that all participants in the debates on WPR application from 1973 to 1980 understood the issue to be not the advisability of the actions in question but rather the nature of the precedent being set. On this level, the Executive position was by far the more successful.

The provisions of the WPR did not, as some as had hoped, become routine procedures followed whenever U.S. troops were deployed abroad. Instead, the burden of proof was shifted to those wishing to invoke the WPR in any given instance. The experience of the 1970s suggested that, in ambiguous cases, their position would be a weak one. In this context, the technical details of the resolution proved to be largely unenforceable; there would be no forward defense of the WPR.

The broader purposes that motivated the authors of the WPR, however, were not abandoned. The resolution, after all, was but one means to a larger end—more effective congressional participation in the entire process of foreign policy decision-making. In the mid- and late-1970s, Congress made considerable progress toward this end, asserting itself in areas that before were the unchallenged realm of the Executive and acquiring the informational and analytic resources to support such initiatives.

CONGRESS AND FOREIGN POLICY IN THE 1970s: A BROADER VIEW

A fuller understanding of congressional behavior and of the institutional environment of the 1970s emerges from a comparison of the Congress' record on implementation of the WPR with its activity in other areas of foreign and military policy during the same period. In general, the 1970s were a decade of exceptional legislative assertiveness in these fields, as Congress significantly expanded its control over such areas as foreign assistance, arms sales, and intelligence activities.

In 1974, less than a year after passage of the WPR, two important measures were enacted that increased congressional influence in two areas of foreign policy not covered by the WPR. The Hughes-Ryan Amendment provided the first attempt since the National Security Act of 1947 to assert a measure of congressional oversight over intelligence agencies and covert military activities, requiring that appropriate committees of Congress be informed of significant covert operations. The Nelson-Bingham Amendment, which dealt with arms sales, went even further, instituting a mechanism by which Congress could move by concurrent resolution to disallow U.S. sales of weapons to foreign countries.

These measures were representative of their revolutionary times as much by the circumstances of their passage as by their content. Both were introduced as floor amendments to the 1974 Foreign Assistance Act (P.L. 93-559), short-circuiting the standing committee and leadership structure.[26] Indeed, both were opposed by much of the established House and Senate leadership. These legislative tactics were reminiscent of the purse-string restrictions passed at the end of the Vietnam War and stood in sharp contrast to the lengthy and methodical legislative history of the WPR.

In addition to passing these amendments, the Congress made its influence felt on foreign policy with two spectacular interventions in 1974 and 1975. The Turkish arms embargo and the Clark Amendment restricting activities in Angola, provided convincing examples (if any were still needed) of the lengths to which Members of Congress were willing to go in order to convince the President and Executive branch officials to treat the Congress as a serious force in foreign policymaking. As such, it is useful to examine these measures in some detail.

The Turkish Arms Embargo

When, in July 1974, a Greek-backed coup on the island of Cyprus led to fighting between the island's Greek and Turkish communities and eventually triggered a Turkish invasion of the island, the United States quickly became deeply involved.[27] As members of NATO, both Greece and Turkey had long-standing security relations with the United States, but strains existed in both cases.

U.S. ties to the military regime that held power in Athens at the outset of the crisis had long been under attack from liberals in the United States, both in and out of Congress. Largely as a result of the Cyprus affair, however, the regime of the "Colonels" collapsed, to be replaced by a civilian government whose political orientation and long-term stability were unclear. This turn of events caused both the Congress and the Ford Administration to be ambivalent and, to a certain degree, confused in their dealings with Athens. Relations with Turkey, meanwhile, deteriorated rapidly as the perception grew in the United States that the Turks had employed excessive force in their intervention and were proving intransigent in the aftermath.

Through Secretary of State Henry Kissinger, the Ford Administration expended considerable effort in attempting to bring about a negotiated settlement to the crisis. In his search for a diplomatic solution, Kissinger dealt directly with Greek and Turkish officials in his well-known, highly personal style. This approach seemed to have failed, however, when talks broke off in August and Turkish forces in Cyprus resumed their offensive, eventually occupying nearly half of the island.

This second invasion mobilized congressional opinion against Turkey. At the same time, Members were increasingly disturbed with what they perceived as the uncooperative attitude of the State Department, and particularly of Secretary Kissinger. Indeed, the question of Kissinger's methods and attitudes became a political issue of equal import with—perhaps eclipsing—the diplomatic and strategic implications of the Cyprus situation in the minds of certain Members of Congress.

By September, sentiment was growing that Congress should take unilateral action and send a message to the Turks and the Executive branch alike. Imposing an arms embargo against Turkey emerged as an effective means both to "punish" Turkey and to respond to what many in Congress considered to be Turkish violation—with the Ford Administration's tacit approval after the fact—of U.S. arms export laws stipulating that U.S.-supplied weapons be used exclusively for defensive purposes.

The arms embargo concept was strongly opposed by the Ford Administration, which wished to retain maximum freedom of action vis-à-vis both Greece and Turkey. The Executive tactics, however, served chiefly to fan the flames of congressional resentment. By seeming to place abstract strategic considerations above congressionally mandated legal requirements, Kissinger and the Ford Administration set themselves directly against the prevailing mood of the Congress. The essential difference in viewpoints between the two branches was captured in one well-known interchange between Secretary Kissinger and Senator Thomas Eagleton (D-MO), who had become a leader of the embargo movement. Responding to Kissinger's assertion that the Congress did not understand foreign policy priorities, the Senator replied simply, "Mr. Secretary, you do not understand the rule of law."[28]

By late September, the issue had degenerated into an open confrontation between Members of Congress and Secretary Kissinger. The first vote on embargo legislation came on September 19, 1974, when a nonbinding resolution introduced by Senator Eagleton proposing that all military aid to Turkey be cut off passed by a vote of 64 to 27. Within days, binding legislation was making its way through both Houses. Following presidential vetoes, which the House of Representatives failed to override, of two embargo bills passed in mid-October, an agreement was finally reached under which the Administration would have until December 10 (later extended to February 5) to pursue negotiations. No tangible results having been reached by that date, the arms embargo provision—ultimately attached to the 1974 Foreign Assistance Act—went into effect.[29]

For the Executive branch, the imposition of the Turkish embargo demonstrated the risk of underestimating the change in congressional attitudes that had occurred in the early 1970s. A majority of Members of Congress, convinced that legislative inaction had contributed to initiating and prolonging the politically discredited Vietnam War, were determined to assert their influence, even if it meant openly opposing not only the Administration but also the established congressional leadership. Embargo supporters concluded that the political mood of the country would enable them to prevail in such a conflict. This assessment proved correct in 1974, and it was reinforced the following year in the context of a very different foreign policy debate.

U.S. Activities in Angola

With the 1975 revelation of the CIA's involvement in the civil war that followed the pull-out of Portuguese forces from Angola, a number of legislators saw an opportunity to assert congressional power over U.S. covert operations. A few Senators, of whom the most influential was Dick Clark (D-IA), chairman of the African Affairs Subcommittee of the Senate Foreign Relations Committee, opposed this policy on substantive grounds, believing the intervention to be unwise and detrimental to the long-term interests of the United States in Africa.[30] This view was also held by certain Administration officials, notably Assistant Secretary of State for African Affairs Nathaniel Davis, who resigned in protest over the issue. It is fair to say, however, that for the majority of Members of Congress, the issue was not Angola but the Administration's attempt to involve the United States in yet another secret war.

The Ford Administration's actions suggest that it understood clearly that in the wake of the fall of South Vietnam, it would be impossible to garner political support for overt military intervention in Africa—thus its decision to employ covert means. Once the operation was revealed, the ensuing political consequences were probably inevitable.

Since no U.S. military forces were involved in the Angola operation, the WPR was not applicable. Accordingly, Members wishing to end the intervention found themselves in the same position as those who had attempted to legislate an end to the Vietnam war five years earlier. Once again, purse-string limitations proved to be the only applicable instrument.

The original measure cutting off funds for intervention in Angola was sponsored by Senator John Tunney (D-CA), who seems to have seized upon the issue chiefly for its political potential.[31] The Tunney Amendment was similar in scope and intent to Eagleton's 1973 Cambodian bombing cutoff. Not only was the defense appropriations bill, to which the measure was attached, reduced by the amount that Tunney estimated was earmarked for Angola, but a provision was added prohibiting any transfer of other funds to carry out covert activities in Angola. The amendment passed by large margins in both the House and Senate, whereupon President Ford evidently concluded that he had little choice but to accept it and end the U.S. covert intervention in Angola.

While the Tunney Amendment applied only to 1976, a series of measures subsequently introduced by Senator Clark prohibited any renewed direct or indirect U.S. involvement with forces seeking to overthrow the Angolan government. The policy of nonintervention in Angola thus came to be known generally as the "Clark Amendment."

Results and Significance of Congressional Activism

The Turkish and Angolan episodes can be considered victories for Congress in its power struggle with the Executive branch during the early 1970s. They are not, however, examples of good foreign policy. Many of the problems identified with the purse-string legislation of the Vietnam era can be seen in these cases as well.

There can be little doubt that the arms embargo greatly hampered U.S. relations with Turkey in the mid-1970s and did not contribute to finding a settlement to the ongoing problems posed by the situation in Cyprus—a source of tension to this day. The diplomatic repercussions of the Angolan affair were not so dramatic; as seen from without, however, U.S. policy in this case appeared, at best, erratic.

On the domestic front, the Executive branch, as well as many outside observers, laid the blame for the less than stellar performance of the United States in these situations squarely on the Congress, ignoring the possibility that a more forthcoming attitude from the Administration and Secretary Kissinger might have avoided the Turkish embargo, while prior consultation with Congress would almost certainly have established that the necessary level of support for the Angolan operation simply did not exist. (The belief that U.S. involvement in Angola could be successfully concealed from the Congress, or anyone else, over the long term stretches the limits of credibility.) In retrospect, it seems more accurate to conclude that the principal problem lay not so much with the objectives and policies of either the legislative or the Executive branch, but rather in the nearly total inability of the two branches to engage in timely and significant communication during this period.

Many individuals in both branches, in fact, recognized the dangers inherent in this situation; the subsequent history of policy toward both Turkey and Angola demonstrates significant, albeit not uniformly successful, efforts at inter-branch cooperation. In the year following the enactment of the arms embargo, the Ford Administration put considerable effort into repairing its relations with Congress on this issue and was rewarded with a partial lifting of the embargo in August 1975. In 1978 the Carter Administration mounted a major legislative campaign that succeeded in having the entire embargo repealed.[32] Having brought Congress into the policy process, these and successive Administrations found the Members to be responsive to the needs and priorities of U.S. diplomacy.

The Angolan case provides an example of actions taken from the Legislative side with similar intentions. The final version of the Clark Amendment (P.L. 96-533, Section 118) addressed a number of the limitations previously encountered by purse-string legislation of this sort. In particular, the amendment set out an explicit procedure by which the President could, if he certified that it were in the national interest to do so, request renewed military assistance for antigovernment forces in Angola.

Upon such a request, Congress, following expedited procedures similar to those of the WPR, would signal its approval or disapproval through a joint resolution. The amount and recipient of the aid would be specified in advance. Rather than prohibiting involvement in Angola outright, these provisions emphasized the necessity of prior congressional consent.[33]

The two branches' increasingly constructive attitude was further illustrated by the enactment of two major pieces of legislation, the Arms Export Control Act of 1976 and the Intelligence Oversight Act of 1980. These laws, which expanded the provisions of the Nelson-Bingham Amendment and the Hughes-Ryan Amendment, respectively, differed both from their legislative precursors and from the WPR in that they were explicitly accepted by the Executive branch after a period of reasonably cordial Legislative-Executive negotiation. The idea that Congress had a significant role to play in the formulation of foreign policy was gaining credibility.

Facilitating this new role was a vast expansion in congressional staff resources and, more generally, in the quality and quantity of information and analysis available to Members of Congress. The 1970s saw the number of Legislative staff personnel increase more than threefold. At the same time, the specialized research and support organizations attached to the Legislative branch, namely the Congressional Budget Office, Congressional Research Service, and General Accounting Office, were reorganized and expanded. By giving Congress independent access to information, these developments enabled members and committees to deal with the Executive branch on a more even basis.[34]

CONCLUSION: THE POLITICS OF WAR POWERS IN THE 1970s

Having observed that attempts to implement various provisions of the WPR during the Ford and Carter Administrations led to ambiguous results at best, while at the same time Congress made substantial progress in asserting its influence in the related fields of arms sales and intelligence activities, it seems reasonable to ask why efforts to expand the congressional role in foreign policymaking met with such inconsistent results. We have already noted that internal problems with the WPR made it difficult to implement. In the larger context suggested above, two additional factors seem to be significant.

First is the potential for congressional enforcement—in practice, its ability to deny funding. Because it relied on the undisputed power of Congress to deny funds unless certain predetermined conditions were met, the Clark Amendment, unlike the WPR, proved to be self-executing. Likewise, the Congress' ability to disallow arms sales stems largely from the fact that such sales typically require U.S. Government financing in the form of grants or loans. Oversight of intelligence activities is possible largely because the House and Senate Intelligence Committees, whose status was confirmed by the Intelligence Oversight Act, have established their right to review and amend the CIA's annual budget.

Significantly, the power of the purse is wielded indirectly in each of these cases. The Arms Export Control Act provides for congressional review of arms sales before they are finalized, avoiding the prospect that Congress might cancel them after contracts have been signed and the good faith of the U.S. Government committed. Similarly, the intelligence committees are able, at least in theory, to review policy before it is put into effect. Such review should lessen the likelihood of misunderstandings typified by the Angola affair. As we shall see, however, a considerable gap remains between this ideal and the role actually played by the intelligence committees; the lessons of Angola had to be relearned in the context of Nicaragua.

The War Powers Resolution, by contrast, failed to establish the link between Congress' ultimate power to terminate certain activities by denying them funding, and its desire to participate in the policy decisions preceding them. Accordingly, Members wishing to implement the resolution's consultation and oversight provisions were forced to rely exclusively on Congress' interpretation of its constitutional rights and prerogatives—a position whose weakness we have observed. The only other alternative is to employ ad hoc purse-string measures such as the Tunney Amendment, also a limited option.

The second factor separating the debates over implementation of the WPR from the other cases we have noted is the question of political visibility. An essential difference between these issues and the application of the WPR was that the former were tied to specific, easily identified, and politically explosive issues such as the Turkish invasion of Cyprus, arms sales to Arab countries, or revelations of U.S. covert involvement in such nations as Chile and Angola. WPR compliance, by contrast, was a largely theoretical issue during the 1970s. The events in question, although important as precedents, were not in and of themselves controversial, or even particularly important.

The attitude of Presidents Ford and Carter ensured that nothing less than an all-out confrontation would succeed in breaking the constitutional impasse over the WPR. Lacking the leverage of political immediacy, congressional proponents of the WPR apparently did not consider themselves in a position to prevail in such a contest. On those issues that were politically visible, however, Members of Congress did not fear confrontation, and prevailed on a number of occasions.

For all of these reasons, the WPR did not immediately become, as Javits and Zablocki had hoped, a mutually acceptable procedural compact between the Executive and Legislative branches. The resolution's significance should not be underestimated, however. For the Executive branch, its continued existence was a reminder of the Congress' desire for a meaningful role in formulating all aspects of foreign policy. For the Legislative branch, the WPR became a part of the formal institutional memory as, at the very least, a clear statement of congressional intent. Finally, the symbolic value of the resolution ensured that it would remain in force, providing a ready, albeit imperfect, vehicle for future action. In the words of long-time opponent Senator John Tower, "The War Powers Act is like motherhood and Sunday School and apple pie, something you just cannot vote against."[35]

II TOWARD A NEW EQUILIBRIUM

4 PRESIDENTIAL INITIATIVES

The election of Ronald Reagan to the Presidency in 1980 altered the political context of Executive-Legislative relations in general and questions of war powers in particular. For the first time in a decade, a strong, popular President was in office; his powers of persuasion over both the Congress and the public proved formidable. At the same time, a narrow but reliable Republican majority in the Senate for the first six years of President Reagan's term ensured that body's support of the President's policies with very few exceptions.

The Democratic majority in the House, meanwhile, was divided. A substantial number of Representatives regularly supported the President's policies, while the Democratic leadership of the House opposed them with only limited success. The leadership's partial resurgence after the midterm elections of 1982 improved coherence and discipline in the House and hardened its stand against the President on certain issues, but this advantage was lost for the two years between the President's landslide reelection in 1984 and the Republicans' loss of the Senate in 1986.

In this context, partisan politics regularly overwhelmed institutional considerations (Democrats vs. Republicans rather than Congress vs. the President). As a result, most Democratic attempts to oppose the President's foreign policy decisions by means of institutionally accepted vehicles, such as funding restrictions, met with no more success than attempts to invoke the WPR in questionable cases. Both tactics were regularly defeated by the President's congressional allies without requiring direct action by the Executive. At the same time, the Reagan Administration made no secret of the fact that it intended to pursue a foreign policy unlike that of its immediate predecessors in methods and priorities. Both as a candidate for the Presidency and as chief executive, Ronald Reagan promised a more aggressive defense of U.S. goals and interests throughout the world, a course that many observers feared would lead to confrontations with foreign powers and the Congress alike.

In fact, as we shall see, the Reagan Administration's foreign policy initiatives, although aggressive by the standards of the Ford and Carter Administrations, were well within the boundaries set by Presidents Johnson and Nixon. More to the point, the new Administration's actions remained, on the whole, within the outer limits of permissibility suggested by the precedents of the 1970s.

Like its predecessors, the Reagan Administration refused to concede the unambiguous constitutionality of the WPR. Like them as well, it nevertheless sought to establish at least a minimum record of compliance with the law. As of 1987 the Reagan Administration had invoked the WPR eight times:[1]

1. Sinai (1982)—deployment of U.S. forces to the Multinational Force and Observers created by the Israeli-Egyptian peace treaty
2. Beirut (1982)—deployment of U.S. Marines to the first Multinational Force supervising the withdrawal of Palestinian forces from Beirut
3. Beirut (1982)—deployment of U.S. troops to the second Beirut Multinational Force
4. Chad (1982)—deployment of AWACS and F-15s to assist the government of Chad against invading Libyan forces
5. Beirut (1983)—report following the first U.S. casualties in Beirut
6. Grenada (1983)—U.S. military actions against the revolutionary government of Grenada
7. Libya (1986)—U.S. air raid against targets in the Libyan cities of Tripoli and Benghazi
8. Persian Gulf (1987)—U.S. naval actions against Iranian positions

Although several of these incidents sparked heated controversy concerning Executive compliance with the terms of the WPR, Congress did not, during this time, make significant progress toward expanding its power beyond the level defined in the late 1970s. It did, however, take action to defend the gains of the previous decade. The Reagan Administration's two most controversial foreign policy actions—the deployment of U.S. forces to Lebanon and the program of assistance to Nicaraguan rebel forces—provoked strong congressional reaction and provided real-world test cases for the theoretical procedures and structures the Congress had established during the 1970s.

On the whole, the Reagan Administration saw both Congress and the Executive branch test and consolidate the powers and prerogatives each had defined theoretically in the previous decade. In this chapter, we examine those cases that were characterized by Executive success and congressional acquiescence. Chapter 5 discusses the events and controversies surrounding U.S. involvement in Lebanon and Nicaragua. By examining and analyzing the interaction of the two branches in these contrasting situations, we can begin to understand the nature of the balance of power that emerged between Congress and the President after the institutional upheavals of the 1970s.

THEORETICAL CONSIDERATIONS

Before examining specific events, it is helpful to take note of some legal and rhetorical developments. Of particular importance are a number of judicial decisions that had bearing on the WPR and initial policy statements from high Administration officials concerning the resolution.

Legal Issues

A series of 1983 Supreme Court decisions regarding the use of so-called legislative vetoes, particularly in the case of *INS* vs. *Chadha*, cast serious doubt on the constitutionality of the concurrent resolution mechanism included in Section 5 of the WPR.[2] The Court's decision in the *Chadha* case dealt with a section of the Immigration and Naturalization Act that allowed either House of Congress to overturn a decision by the Attorney General to suspend the deportation of an alien. Writing for the Court majority, Chief Justice Warren Burger asserted that such congressional action constituted "legislation" and, accordingly, "requires action in conformity with the express procedures of the Constitution's prescriptions for legislative action: passage by a majority of both Houses and presentation to the President."[3] A subsequent Court decision, handed down in the *F.T.C.* case, confirmed that this rule also applied to cases in which both Houses acted by means of a concurrent resolution.[4]

In essence, the Court's decisions in these cases seemed to imply that once Congress granted the Executive branch authority over a particular matter, that authority could be rescinded, either in total or for a specific instance, only by new affirmative legislation. In the wake of these decisions, many observers concluded that Section 5(c) of the WPR, which allows Congress to terminate a presidentially initiated military operation by concurrent resolution, would be invalidated. While legal scholars and Members of Congress are not unanimous on this point, the practical effect of the *Chadha* and *F.T.C.* cases was to shift the status of Section 5(c) from highly controversial to essentially unenforceable.

Recognizing this situation, Senator Robert Byrd (D-WV) introduced legislation in 1983 to amend the WPR by substituting a joint resolution for the concurrent resolution provided for in Section 5(c), thus conforming with the Court's ruling that all legislative acts be presented to the President for signature. The Senate approved Byrd's amendment by a vote of 86 to 11 on October 20, 1983, but no such legislation was passed by the House. The issue was ultimately resolved in the House-Senate conference on the State Department Authorization Bill, to which Byrd's amendment was attached. At that time, it was decided not to amend the WPR, but rather to substitute freestanding legislation providing for expedited procedures similar to those of the WPR for any bill or joint resolution mandating the removal of armed forces engaged in hostilities abroad in the absence of a declaration of war or other specific statutory authorization.[5]

By adopting this course, Senator Byrd and his allies accomplished the necessary changes in the law with a minimum of controversy. In particular, they avoided reopening debate on the WPR itself. Moreover, passage of this legislation (P.L. 98-164) did not constitute a formal recognition that Section 5(c) of the WPR was invalid; rather it left open the theoretical possibility that subsequent legal or legislative actions might, at some point, revalidate the concurrent resolution mechanism. For all practical purposes, however, the Byrd Amendment superseded Section 5(c) of the WPR.

In practice, it is possible that this move may actually have strengthened the WPR's legal position by definitively replacing the most suspect portion and thus freeing the rest from guilt by association. Although of considerable potential and theoretical significance, however, this issue is not directly relevant to any of the actual instances of WPR application during the Reagan Administration, since the procedure in Section 5(c) was never attempted.

Attempts to force a broader judicial test of the WPR did not lead to any definitive conclusion concerning the resolution's constitutionality. In 1981 Congressman George Crockett (D-MI) and twenty-eight colleagues initiated legal action against the Reagan Administration for violation of the WPR with regard to activities in El Salvador. The Superior Court of the District of Columbia, however, ruled that Congress, not the courts, was responsible for establishing whether the President was in compliance with the law in this instance. In defending this position, Judge Joyce Green pointed out that the Congress had available to it numerous legislative and investigative options, which it had not chosen to employ.[6] A similar lawsuit brought by a group of Members in the context of the 1987 Persian Gulf operations met with the same response.[7]

The rulings in these cases suggested that the judiciary would treat specific cases of WPR applicability as political questions and refuse to rule on them. Neither the Congress nor the Executive branch, meanwhile, demonstrated particular eagerness to submit the general issue of the WPR's constitutionality to a judicial decision.

Administration Positions

The Reagan Administration's initial position on the question of the constitutionality and applicability of the WPR was remarkably positive. In his confirmation hearings before the Senate Foreign Relations Committee, Secretary of State designate Alexander Haig declared, "I think that the President has an obligation . . . if he were to move, heaven forbid, to introduce American forces into conflict to notify Congress immediately, *and the Congress has the right within 60 to 90 days to overrule that decision.*" (emphasis added)[8]

While not an affirmative endorsement of the entire WPR, this statement, more than any other by a high official of the Executive branch, approached recognizing the applicability of Section 5. Interestingly, Haig's stated rationale for this position paralleled the reasoning of the WPR's conservative supporters of a decade earlier. Again speaking at his confirmation hearing, he said: "Heaven help us as a nation if we once again indulge in the expenditure of precious American blood without a clear demonstration of popular support for it. I think the legislature is the best manifestation of popular support."[9] It is notable that the only WPR report submitted during Secretary Haig's tenure, which related to the noncontroversial deployment of U.S. troops to the Multinational Force in the Sinai in March 1982, was also the only report submitted by President Reagan that specifically cited the relevant section of the WPR, in this case Section 4(a)(2).

Other Administration officials, at least on the rhetorical level, seemed to recognize and accept the changed institutional environment. Secretary of Defense Caspar Weinberger, speaking in 1984, voiced sentiments much like those of conservative backers of war powers legislation in the early 1970s: "Before the U.S. commits combat forces abroad, there must be some reasonable assurance that we will have the support of the American people and their elected representatives in Congress. We cannot fight a battle with Congress at home while asking our troops to win a war overseas."[10]

In contrast to statements such as these, the public positions taken by Secretary of State George Shultz mirrored the analysis of Administration legal advisors in the Nixon and Ford years. When questioned on this issue during his 1982 confirmation hearings by Senator Percy, Shultz was willing to state only that "the Administration has every intention of complying fully with the consulting and reporting requirements of the WPR," pointedly omitting any mention of the oversight provisions of Section 5.[11] Shultz's later statements were more directly critical and tended to be echoed by other State Department officials.

BRIEF MILITARY OPERATIONS: GRENADA AND LIBYA

The Reagan Administration replaced the theoretical precedents and definitional reinterpretations of the Ford and Carter years—which comprised the WPR's case law record—with concrete actions, testing the limits of the President's effective freedom of action. The war powers controversies of the Ford and Carter Administrations fell into a general pattern. The President, acting on his self-defined authority as commander-in-chief, would initiate a military action that, by virtue of its suddenness and brevity, had ended before the Congress had time to respond. This was true both of the cases when the WPR was formally invoked and of others, such as the Zaire airlift, when it was not. Moreover, in most instances the popularity of the President's action did much to deter any serious effort to hold him accountable for deviations from strict application of the WPR. Two of President Reagan's most spectacular military initiatives, the 1983 invasion of Grenada and the 1986 actions against Libya, expanded on this pattern.

When President Reagan ordered U.S. forces to invade Grenada in 1983, triggering the most intense military action undertaken by the United States since the end of the Vietnam War, he claimed to be acting strictly on his authority as commander-in-chief. In a further parallel to events of the 1970s, Reagan justified his action chiefly as a mission to rescue U.S. civilians endangered by revolutionary violence. Similarly, the August 1986 bombing of Tripoli and Benghazi was a sudden and discrete action. In this case, however, there was not even a pretext of rescuing U.S. citizens; the Libyan air raid was openly acknowledged to be a punitive, or at best a preemptive, action taken to counter Libyan backing of terrorist groups.

The obvious difference between President Reagan's actions and those of his predecessors was, of course, one of scale. Would this increase in magnitude have a significant effect on congressional reactions, and might the political outcome of the debates following these events indicate the practical limits to presidentially initiated military initiatives of this sort? The Grenada invasion, for one example, suggested that these limits might be quite broad indeed.

The Invasion of Grenada

Relations between the United States and Grenada had been extremely poor since the 1979 coup that brought Maurice Bishop and his left-wing New Jewel Movement to power. Both the Carter and Reagan Administrations were critical of the Bishop government, noting its close ties to Cuba and the Soviet Union. Beyond such ideological considerations, a concrete point of contention between Grenada and the United States arose with the construction of the Point Salines Airport, which began in 1980 with aid from the World Bank and West European countries, as well as from Cuba and the Soviet Union. According to the government of Grenada and the project's Western sponsors, the airfield was intended to provide the island with a modern airport capable of handling international air traffic, a facility it had previously lacked. The U.S. Government charged, however, that the airfield would in reality be used as a military base for Soviet and Cuban aircraft.[12]

In light of the Reagan Administration's dislike of the Bishop government, it is ironic that the immediate cause of the U.S. invasion was Bishop's overthrow on October 13, 1983. The impetus for the coup seems to have come from far-left elements in Bishop's government, but the original instigators soon lost control of the situation. On October 19, Army Commander General Hudson Austin proclaimed himself to be the leader of a military governing council, although it is not clear that he exercised control over anything other than the armed forces.

Grenada's island neighbors feared that a government even more radical than Bishop's would emerge and make Grenada a base for Cuban-backed subversion in the eastern Caribbean. By October 19, the Barbados government had claimed publicly that it would consider military intervention in Grenada if unspecified other nations would also participate. According to subsequent press reports, negotiations concerning U.S. participation in such an operation may have been underway as early as October 15.

The first reported high-level U.S. action on this issue, however, was a meeting of Reagan Administration security officials, chaired by Vice President George Bush and including Secretary of State Shultz, on October 20. At the meeting, the officials decided to divert a navy/marine task force bound for Lebanon to the Caribbean. Publicly they cited ensuring the safety of American citizens in Grenada as the reason for this action, although no specific mission seems to have been defined at the time. The move seemed purely precautionary and resembled past U.S. actions that had not resulted in military intervention.

A second meeting was held two days later to consider a formal request for U.S. military assistance made by eight Caribbean nations, including Barbados and Jamaica. After this meeting, Secretary Shultz stated that the President was "willing to consider" military action in Grenada, and U.S. and Caribbean officials began making military contingency plans. By October 23, President Reagan was reported by Shultz to have made a tentative decision to proceed with an invasion. The President made his decision formal on the evening of October 24.[13]

The initial invasion was made by a force of 1,900 U.S. troops, consisting of marines from the navy task force who had been diverted to Grenada on October 20, as well as Army Ranger forces and elements of the 82nd airborne division. Upon encountering unexpectedly strong resistance from Grenadan and Cuban troops, the United States sent in additional units of the 82nd airborne division as reinforcements. At its height, the U.S. contingent was reported to have to have reached 6,000 combatants, supported by helicopters and carrier-based air strikes.[14] Major fighting lasted into the fourth day after the invasion, and scattered incidents broke out for nearly a week thereafter.

Considering the magnitude and deliberateness of the U.S. action, there can be no doubt that all aspects of the WPR—consultation, reporting, and oversight—applied to the Grenada invasion. Administration compliance, however, can most generously be described as minimal. President Reagan did submit a report to Congress on October 25, the day following the invasion, describing his actions as "consistent" with the WPR but citing no particular subsection, thereby avoiding any implication that the President might ultimately be bound by any of the resolution's provisions.[15] After the 1975 *Mayaguez* incident, the occasion that most closely resembled the Grenada case, President Ford had specifically cited Section 4(a)(1). Reagan's failure to do so in this case, given the obvious existence of "hostilities" even by previous Administrations' definitions, was thus a step backward from the established level of compliance.

Two principal points of contention emerged during the congressional debate that followed: (1) whether the President had fulfilled the consultation requirement of Section 3 of the WPR, and (2) whether the Administration would be bound by the sixty-day limit on troop deployments set in Section 5.

On the issue of prior consultation, it is fairly clear that the Administration acted on the narrowest possible interpretation of the law. Reagan did brief Senators Howard Baker and Robert Byrd and Congressmen Tip O'Neill, James Wright, and Robert Michel on the evening of the invasion, but the congressional participants later agreed that they were informed rather than consulted. O'Neill: "We weren't asked for advice . . . we were informed what was taking place"; Baker: "We were not consulted in the sense that there was no solicitation of opinion"; Byrd: "The Administration only tells the Senate after it makes its decision . . . it does not ask for the advice of the Senate." Supporting these claims was the fact, established soon after the invasion, that the President had signed the official order to invade before his meeting with the Members of Congress.[16]

Speaking for the Administration in hearings before the Senate Foreign Relations Committee, Deputy Secretary of State Kenneth Dam asserted that earlier or more extensive consultation would have been impossible for security reasons.[17] Objective examination, however, suggests otherwise. Even if one grants, for the sake of argument, the Administration's implicit assertion that consultation with Congress would automatically result in a breach of security, the Grenada operation was by no means a closely held secret.

A U.S.-backed military intervention in Grenada had been proposed openly by the governments of Barbados and several other Caribbean states at a special meeting of the Caribbean Common Market held on October 22. The ensuing debate was widely reported in the Caribbean press. Moreover, Grenadan and Cuban leaders seem to have been fully aware of U.S. intentions. The sailing and destination of the U.S. task force, and the associated possibility of a U.S. invasion, were general knowledge in the Caribbean from at least October 22; the Grenadan armed forces were on full alert as of the following day;[18] and reinforcements and equipment are known to have arrived in Grenada from Cuba at least twenty-four hours before the U.S. invasion.[19]

In a post-invasion interview, General Wesley McDonald, commander of U.S. forces in the Atlantic region, acknowledged that the Cuban government was aware that "U.S. intervention was likely" and had taken effective action to prepare for it.[20] Indeed, one report suggests that the U.S. State Department itself may have informed the Cuban government hours before the invasion that the imminent U.S. military action in Grenada did not threaten Cuban civilians on the island.[21] In this context, it is difficult to imagine what harm might have been done to security if selected Members of Congress had been consulted early enough for a meaningful exchange of views to take place.

Mr. Dam further justified Reagan's actions by asserting that although the order for the invasion had indeed been signed before the President had consulted with congressional leaders, it could have been countermanded if the opposition of congressional leaders had so warranted.[22] Since the Members consulted in fact made no attempt to oppose the President, it is impossible to know what the result of such opposition might have been. Realistically, however, it is difficult to imagine that congressional leaders, called in at the last moment to discuss an issue for which they were unprepared, and confronted with the various information sources of the Executive branch, could make the sort of vigorous opposition that might give a President pause. It was precisely this sort of situation that the authors of the WPR were trying to replace with a workable procedure when they wrote Section 3. In any case, the question of consultation was moot by the time congressional committees met to debate the issue.

A more important practical question concerned the role to be played by Congress after the operation was underway. No one denied that the situation in Grenada qualified as hostile—even Deputy Secretary Dam admitted that "as a factual matter, there were hostilities there." However, he refused to consider the applicability of Section 5(b). Noting that all Administrations since 1973 had "constitutional problems" with the sixty-day cutoff, he gave the Administration's view that it would be "unwise to discuss what the constitutional situation would be if hostilities were still going on after 60 days." Such an extension of U.S. activities, Dam assured the committee, was unlikely to happen, "so I don't think we'll have a problem here."[23]

Given this less than forthcoming attitude on the part of its spokesman, the Administration's failure to cite Section 4(a)(1) of the WPR in its report could be interpreted as a renewed assertion that the President was not ultimately bound by Section 5. If this position were to be challenged, it would first be necessary to establish unambiguously that the conditions set forth in Section 4(a)(1) had been met. Both the House and the Senate moved quickly to implement the operative provisions of the War Powers Resolution.

After a brief hearing, the House Foreign Affairs Committee reported back a resolution (H.J.Res. 402, 98th Cong.) stating that the requirements of Section 4(a)(1) had been met and that the countdown toward the sixty-day limit had begun on October 25.[24] This resolution passed the full house by a bipartisan vote of 403 to 23 on November 1.

In the Senate, a similar resolution (S.J.Res. 186, 98th Cong.) was introduced by Senator Gary Hart (D-CO) on October 26, but was not acted upon by the Foreign Relations Committee, to which it was referred. On the 28th, Senator Hart reintroduced the legislation, this time as an amendment to the debt limit bill then pending (H.R. 308, 98th Cong.). In debate on the Senate floor, opponents of the Hart Amendment spoke both against the constitutionality of the WPR itself (Senator Barry Goldwater) and in support of the President's actions from a political and security, rather than legal, viewpoint (Senators Steve Symms [R-ID] and Pete Wilson [R-CA]). Even opponents of the President's action, such as Senator Lowell Weicker (R-CT) tended to ignore the legal issue of WPR compliance and focus their remarks on the merits of the Grenada invasion.[25] Senator Paul Sarbanes (D-MD), speaking for the amendment, attempted to focus the issue in question: "At issue is not the wisdom of the President's action. . . . The issue is whether the Executive alone will make the decision as to continued involvement or must he come to Congress and obtain the judgment of Congress."[26] Despite the general lack of enthusiasm, however, most Senators seem eventually to have concluded that the undeniable existence of hostilities in this case left them little choice but to acknowledge that the conditions set out in Section 4(a)(1) had been met, and the Hart Amendment was adopted by a bipartisan vote of 64 to 20.

Regardless of its passage by a sizable majority, the Hart Amendment was not included in the version of the debt limit bill reported back from conference on November 17. The stated reason for this was that the bill had encountered complications of its own that had delayed its passage beyond the time when the government was technically without spending authority, and thus urgently needed to be passed expeditiously, without the possible further complications of extraneous amendments. The strong implication, however, is that the Republican Senate leadership was reluctant to pass any measure critical of the President's successful and popular initiative. While they did not actively oppose the Hart Amendment, the leadership also did nothing to rescue it from its final demise.

In an attempt to salvage at least a symbolic victory, Senator Byrd pointed out that both Houses of Congress had passed separate but identically worded legislation "finding" that Section 4(a)(1) applied to the Grenada situation.[27] Even if binding legislation had been passed, however, it is not clear that it would have been accepted by the President. Questioned on this issue by Congressman Gerry Studds (D-MA), Deputy Secretary Dam refused to affirm either that the President would sign H.J.Res. 402, should it reach his desk, or that he would consider himself bound by the sixty-day limit in any circumstances.[28]

In many ways, the invasion of Grenada was a larger scale version of the *Mayaguez* incident. In both cases, the factors contributing to the President's political success are fairly obvious. The rescue of U.S. citizens is, of course, always well received. Moreover, both actions provided a visible example of a U.S. military victory—or at least the plausible perception of such—at a time when preceding events (the final collapse of South Vietnam in 1975 and the bombing of the U.S. Marine headquarters in Beirut in October 1983) had raised considerable public concern about America's military "impotence." Finally, both incidents provided opportunities to strike, albeit indirectly, at popularly perceived "villains"—Vietnam in 1975 and Cuba in 1986.

Congressional reactions were also strikingly parallel. Both actions were widely supported by Members of Congress for many of the same reasons that accounted for their popularity with the electorate at large. In both cases, the imperfect application of the consultation requirements of the WPR and the Administration's ultimate refusal to accept theoretical limits on the commander-in-chief's power were noted and criticized by individual Members, but no concrete steps were taken either to restrain the Administration in the case at hand or to ensure future compliance.

With the Grenada invasion, the Reagan Administration increased the scale of unilateral presidential actions by a full order of magnitude; thousands, rather than hundreds, of U.S. troops were involved. More important, the goal of the operation included bringing about a change of government in the target state, in addition to rescuing U.S. citizens. By dealing with the Grenada invasion much as it had with the *Mayaguez* incident, Congress implicitly recognized a significant increase in the scale of possible presidential initiatives in the post-Vietnam era.

U.S. Actions against Libya

With its efforts to put military pressure on Libya, which culminated in the 1986 air raid against Libyan military facilities near Tripoli and Benghazi, the Reagan Administration forged a precedent for another expansion of the President's recognized area of freedom of action. In this case, the expansion was not of scale but of purpose; retaliation against states sponsoring terrorism was added to the rescue of U.S. citizens as cause for unilateral military action by the President.

Tension between Libya and the United States had long been escalating. A continuing source of the friction was Colonel Muammar al Qadhafi's 1973 declaration that the Gulf of Sidra, off the northern coast of Libya, was part of his country's territorial waters. The United States demonstrated its rejection of this claim by deploying naval units in the area for periodic "freedom of navigation exercises." Although Libya met most of these actions only with verbal protests, in August 1981 two Libyan aircraft were shot down by U.S. jets when they attempted to attack U.S. forces. The Libyan government had previously declared that it would attack foreign units in what it considered to be its territorial waters, but the attack was largely unexpected and apparently not intentionally provoked. (Freedom of navigation exercises are held regularly by the U.S. Navy in a number of critical areas, including waters near the Soviet Union.) Accordingly, there was little domestic opposition to the Reagan Administration's claim that the U.S. forces had acted in self-defense while engaged in legitimate activities in international waters.

U.S.-Libyan relations deteriorated further during the 1980s, as the U.S. government saw increasing evidence that Colonel Qadhafi was providing financial and logistical assistance to terrorist groups whose victims included Americans. The U.S. Government responded by seeking to put diplomatic and economic pressure on Libya, but these tactics were not demonstrably successful.

Libyan-backed terrorist activities continued with a series of spectacular attacks including the December 27, 1985, airport bombings in Rome and

Vienna (killing five Americans).[29] Following these incidents, U.S. forces began a series of large-scale naval operations off the Libyan coast that included periodic transits of the Libyan-claimed Gulf of Sidra. While Administration spokesmen denied that the United States was planning military operations against Libya, these exercises were clearly intended as more than training missions for U.S. forces. On March 24, 1986, Libyan forces responded to the American presence by launching air- and ground-based missiles at U.S. aircraft. In skirmishes over the course of the following days, several Libyan aircraft and gunboats were destroyed, along with ground-based missile and radar sites.[30]

The circumstances of this latest clash prompted certain congressional leaders to question the Administration's assertion that the WPR did not apply to it. In a letter to the President, Congressman Dante Fascell (D-FL) asserted that the Administration had failed to comply with the consultation provisions of the WPR in this case. While reaction to the actual Libyan attacks arguably left no time for consultation, Fascell argued that the consultation should have preceded the initial deployment of U.S. forces: "As demonstrated by today's reported attack, these deployments constituted from the outset a situation where imminent involvement in hostilities was a distinct possibility clearly indicated by the circumstances even prior to today's development."[31]

At the very least, Fascell concluded, the President should submit a report under the WPR. President Reagan did send a report to both Houses of Congress on March 26, but he cited only his "desire that Congress be informed" and made no mention of the WPR.[32] Defending the Administration's position, presidential assistant William Bell III asserted that the operations conducted in the Gulf of Sidra did not place U.S. forces in a condition of actual or imminent hostilities and that merely the "distinct possibility" of hostilities was not sufficient to warrant applying the WPR.[33]

Fascell's position, very much in the spirit of the framers of the WPR, played only a minor role in the political debate over the President's initiatives against Libya. Vastly more important was the widespread congressional and public support for the President's declared stance of "getting tough" with terrorists and their sponsors. Indeed, the Administration was frequently criticized for not taking strong enough actions against such groups.

Libyan-connected terrorist incidents did not end after the March clash with U.S. forces. A bomb attack in a Berlin discotheque on the night of April 5, 1986, left one American dead and some sixty injured. U.S. response was not long in coming.

On the night of April 15, U.S. aircraft based in Great Britain joined with carrier-based aircraft from U.S. ships in the Mediterranean for a series of aerial attacks on military installations near the Libyan cities of Tripoli and Benghazi. Speaking on national television two hours after the attack, President Reagan announced that the United States had "precise, direct and irrefutable evidence" of Libyan involvement in the Berlin bombing.[34] The next day, the President submitted to Congress a report, "consistent with the War Powers Resolution," concerning the action taken against Libya. The report cited Article 51 of the United Nations Charter, which accepts nations' rights of self-defense, as well as the President's authority as commander-in-chief. The U.S. actions were characterized as preemptive strikes against the Libyan terrorist infrastructure, intended to head off any further Libyan-backed terrorist action against Americans.[35]

As in the case of Grenada, the President's consultation with Congress had been, at best, minimal. A group of congressional leaders, including Senators Dole, Byrd, Pell, and Lugar and Congressmen Fascell, Broomfield, and Michel, was briefed at the White House approximately three hours before the attack, but well after the participating aircraft were en route to their targets (Congressmen O'Neill and Wright had been invited but were unable to attend).

Once again, concern was raised about the lack of meaningful consultation. In the words of Congressman Fascell, "We went down [to the White House] at four p.m. and we were told, 'gentlemen, you will be happy to know a decision has been made, planes are in the air.'"[36] For Congressman Fascell, the fact that the attacking aircraft could, in theory, have been called back was largely irrelevant; brought in only at the moment of crisis, the congressional leaders were in no position to assess the Administration's decision, let alone to reverse it.

It would be much more useful, suggested Fascell in a subsequent congressional hearing, for the President to consult with congressional leaders well in advance of deciding to engage U.S. forces in hostilities so that options and priorities could be discussed and evaluated before action was taken.[37] The Administration's representative, State Department Legal

Advisor Abraham Sofaer, expressed no opposition to this suggestion, but there is no indication that the Reagan Administration, or the Congress for that matter, made any move to implement it.

Ironically, the only formal legislative proposal to be inspired by the Libyan raid was a bill submitted by Senate Majority Leader Robert Dole that would have waived the consultation and oversight provisions of the WPR in cases involving "terrorist activity" and extended the reporting deadline in such cases from forty-eight hours to ten days (S. 2335, 99th Cong.).[38] The most frequent justification for such legislation was the fear that consultation with Congress would result—or, indeed, had resulted—in serious breaches of security, even if no intentional leaks occurred. Testifying before the Foreign Relations Committee, Mr. Sofaer suggested that the very act of consultation before the April 15 raid had led to dangerous speculation by the U.S. press.[39] It is not clear, however, why security problems would be more severe in terrorist cases than in any other military situation.

While Dole's proposal never reached a congressional vote, it reflected a substantial body of opinion which held that terrorism constituted a special case that warranted waiving part or all of the WPR.[40] This belief may, in fact, threaten congressional war powers in ways other than by fueling the debate over security. *Terrorism* is a notoriously ill-defined term. Numerous international actors use it to describe their enemies' actions, whatever form those might take. Accordingly, introducing a reference to terrorism into the WPR (which, as we have seen, is already well stocked with definitional ambiguities) would risk providing prior sanction to Executive initiatives far more sweeping than intended by the proponents of Dole's amendment—assuming, of course, that they were not using the catchword *terrorism* as a pretext for undermining the WPR in general. In any case, the military and political success of President Reagan's action against Libya would seem to argue against the position that the WPR restricts the Executive unduly.

Conclusions

The Libyan raid, like the invasion of Grenada, illustrates the realm within which the President can take unilateral military action without incurring effective congressional sanction. Two key factors, one technical and one political, define the area of presidential free action as demonstrated by these events. On the technical level, the WPR, relying as it does on sanctions after the fact, is not an effective instrument for exercising congressional control over military activities lasting only a few hours or, at most, a few days. Experience indicates that the suddenness of these actions renders a consultation requirement unenforceable, while their brevity makes oversight largely irrelevant.

At the same time, the Reagan Administration's actions against Libya and Grenada reinforce a political lesson of the 1970s. When faced with a military initiative whose goals are widely popular and which is initially perceived as having been militarily successful, Congress is not in a position to force a conflict over strict compliance with the WPR. Knowing this, many Members are deterred from even attempting such a course. Symbolic invocation of the WPR, such as was done following the Grenada invasion, probably represents the effective limit of congressional action. This state of affairs had, in fact, been conceded in so many words in a remarkably candid statement by the Senate Foreign Relations Committee in 1982:

> In practice, the [War Powers] Resolution has been interpreted to allow Presidential combat initiatives under virtually any circumstances subject only to the 60-day limit on such activity (without further Congressional authorization) unless Congress vetoes the operation within a shorter period. Even the requirement for prior consultation with Congress "in every possible instance" has been interpreted flexibly.[41]

It is significant, nevertheless, that the Reagan Administration, like its predecessors, carefully defined its policy in such a way as to avoid serious conflicts with the terms of the WPR. All U.S. combat forces were withdrawn from Grenada and Libya well before the sixty-day limit on presidential authorization. Notably, in the case of Grenada, when the extent of U.S. involvement was initially unclear, Administration spokesmen announced from the outset that all U.S. forces would be withdrawn before sixty days.

The Administration's insistence on the point is a clear indication that the limits set out in the WPR were recognized. It is not clear that fear of congressional opposition was the principal motivating factor in the Administration's decision, but the fact remains that the Administration's self-imposed constraints during this period corresponded generally to the outer limits of acceptable U.S. activities established in the WPR.

PROLONGED LOW-LEVEL MILITARY PRESENCE: CENTRAL AMERICA

A different test of the limits of presidential freedom of action was provided by the Reagan Administration's policy in Central America. In this area, the Administration established and maintained a U.S. military presence over periods of months and even years without acknowledging the applicability of the WPR. Military advisors were sent to train and support the armed forces of friendly states in Central America, while large-scale military exercises in Honduras were undertaken to put political and military pressure on the government of Nicaragua. Unlike the incidents cited in the preceding section, these initiatives did not involve U.S. forces in serious hostilities. Nevertheless, they did raise important questions of WPR applicability.

U.S. Advisors in El Salvador

Leftist opposition to the military government of the small Central American nation of El Salvador, long endemic, flared into a major insurgency in the early 1980s. In 1981, the newly elected Reagan Administration responded by requesting a major increase in U.S. economic and military assistance to the Salvadoran government and increased the number of U.S. military advisors in that nation from nineteen to fifty-four. These moves generated considerable public controversy and were challenged by several Members of Congress, principally liberal Democrats.

Opponents of the President's policy criticized U.S. support for what they called a corrupt and brutal regime. The highly publicized murder of U.S. church workers in El Salvador, apparently by Salvadoran security forces, fueled this sentiment in the United States. At the same time, many U.S. observers both in and out of Congress saw the increase in the number of U.S. advisors as the first step in a Vietnam-like military entanglement in Central America. The WPR, a direct product of the Vietnam experience, seemed to be an obvious vehicle for opposing the Administration's policy. On March 3, 1981, Congressman Richard Ottinger (D-NY) and forty-four colleagues sent a telegram to President Reagan stating their belief that sending U.S. advisors to El Salvador required a report under the WPR. The next day, Ottinger introduced a resolution to the same effect in the House of Representatives; Senator Thomas Eagleton did the same in the Senate on March 17.[42]

Although this legislation was never voted on by either House, it did spark congressional debate and hearings. To counter attempts to invoke the WPR, supporters of the Administration's policy sought a clear official statement defining the role of U.S. personnel in El Salvador. In response to a request by Congressman William Broomfield (R-MI), the ranking Republican Member of the House Foreign Affairs Committee, the State Department provided its official opinion that the WPR did not apply to U.S. activities in El Salvador for three reasons: (1) U.S. personnel did not accompany Salvadoran troops into combat; (2) conditions in the areas where U.S. personnel were based, which the Administration described as "irregular or infrequent violence such as sporadic terrorist activity which happens to occur in a particular area," did not constitute "actual or imminent hostilities"; and (3) U.S. personnel carried only personal side arms and thus were not "equipped for combat" within the meaning of the WPR.[43]

Responding to a request for further clarifications from Foreign Affairs Committee Chairman Zablocki, Assistant Secretary of State Richard Fairbanks stated that, while the Administration did not believe that the presence and activities of U.S. personnel in El Salvador required a report under the terms of the WPR, the U.S. Embassy in San Salvador would be "reminded" of the reporting and consulting requirements if these should become applicable at some future time. Further, the Administration agreed to supply periodic voluntary reports on the general status and activities of U.S. advisors in El Salvador.[44] These assurances quieted serious congressional opposition for the rest of 1981.

The Administration's claims that U.S. advisors did not accompany Salvadoran troops into conflict areas and were not equipped for combat within the meaning of the WPR were again brought into question in the spring of 1982 when three U.S. soldiers were photographed by U.S. journalists in combat gear. This incident did not become a serious issue, however, as the Administration explained that the soldiers had acted outside their guidelines, and removed them from El Salvador.[45]

A potentially more serious issue arose when it was reported that the U.S. Army commander in El Salvador had recommended hostile fire pay for U.S. personnel in the country. In a March 1982 Senate Foreign Relations Committee hearing, General Ernest Graves, director of the Defense Security Assistance Agency, stated that this recommendation was due to the possibility of terrorist activity in El Salvador, and that it did not imply that "significant hostilities" as stated in the WPR were underway.[46] Although a number of Senators, particularly John Glenn (D-OH) and Joseph Biden (D-DE), expressed dissatisfaction with this view, the question was not pursued.[47]

Later that summer, a General Accounting Office (GAO) report confirmed that U.S. Army personnel routinely received hostile fire pay based on the army's determination that they were exposed to or in the immediate vicinity of hostile fire, and thus subject to a high risk of casualty. The GAO concluded that such conditions indeed qualified as significant hostilities and, accordingly, that a report under the WPR should be submitted.[48] Since hearings had already been held, however, the report did not lead to further congressional action.

The failure of congressional attempts to invoke the WPR in the case of El Salvador convinced some in Congress that the resolution was inherently inadequate. The ultimate outcome of an attempt by Senate Minority Leader Robert Byrd to strengthen the WPR illustrated instead the overwhelming importance of political, rather than institutional, considerations at that time.

Senate War Powers Debates in 1982

In February 1982 Senator Byrd introduced an amendment to the WPR that would have prohibited the introduction of U.S. armed forces into El Salvador without specific congressional authorization, thereby creating an exception to the sixty-day period of presidential initiative provided by the resolution.[49]

Byrd's testimony to the Foreign Relations Committee in support of his proposal shows that, in addition to questioning the wisdom of the President's Central American policies, he was concerned that the Congress was once again abdicating all of its war powers responsibility. In the case of Vietnam, Byrd reminded the committee, "the issue involved the commitment of U.S. military forces, little by little and then more and more, exclusively by the President allegedly under his power as Commander-in-Chief, without Congressional authorization or adequate consultation with Congress."[50] This pattern was being repeated in El Salvador, Byrd asserted, and the consequences could be equally catastrophic. Moreover, existing vehicles for congressional participation in decisions on war and peace, including the WPR, had proven inadequate.

> The only option open to us at present is a response after the fact. I argue strongly that it is our constitutional responsibility to err on the side of debate and caution before we are confronted with a situation that could cost us so dearly in money, national unity, and the spilling of American blood.[51]

Byrd's proposed response was to strengthen the WPR by eliminating the possibility that troops might be introduced even for less than sixty days in the country where such a move was considered to be most likely.

In essence, Byrd was attempting to return, in this particular case, to the spirit of the original Senate version of the WPR, which would have enumerated the cases in which the President could employ military force unilaterally and required him to seek prior congressional approval in all other cases. This was a much more radical, and accordingly controversial, redefinition of the commander-in-chief's power than that contained in the WPR as passed, which relied chiefly on sanctions after the fact. That battle, however, had been fought and lost in 1973, and the probability of its being won in the vastly different political environment of the 1980s was nil. In any case, Byrd's highly specific provision would have made an incongruous addition to the otherwise generic WPR. The Foreign Relations Committee gave Byrd's amendment a polite hearing but never seriously considered approving it.

Supporters of an active U.S. role in Central America responded to Byrd's challenge when Senator Symms introduced the language of the 1962 Cuba Resolution calling for the United States to ". . . prevent by whatever means may be necessary, including the use of arms, the Marxist-Leninist regime in Cuba from extending by force or threat of force its aggressive or subversive activities to any part of this hemisphere . . ." as a substitute for Byrd's bill. On April 14, 1982, the Senate voted against immediate passage of the Symms Amendment—although by a margin of only two votes—referring it instead to the Foreign Relations Committee, which had already agreed to consider Byrd's measure as well as others concerning El Salvador.[52]

Senator Symms' proposal found little support among the Members of the Foreign Relations Committee, with the notable exception of Senator Jesse Helms (R-NC). After a series of hearings, the committee adopted a compromise resolution proposed by Senator Charles Percy (R-IL). The Percy Amendment provided a strong statement of the U.S. intention to resist Soviet and Cuban-backed aggression throughout the Western Hemisphere without, at the same time, abandoning Congress' right to participate in any future decision to employ military force to that end. While rejecting the idea of amending the WPR along the lines proposed by Senator Byrd, the Percy Amendment emphasized that the commitment of U.S. troops to combat would require specific statutory authorization under the terms of the WPR, which authorization the amendment stated explicitly that it did not provide.[53]

In the report accompanying this measure, the Foreign Relations Committee gave its interpretation of the relevance of the WPR to the ongoing events in Central America, as well as to attempts, such as that by Senator Symms, to make broad statements of U.S. willingness to employ military force.

> The (1962) Cuban Resolution was the product of an earlier era and a different attitude on the part of most members of Congress towards the power to make war on behalf of the United States. Open-ended mandates for the use of force . . . were superseded by the War Powers Resolution in which Congress—by extraordinary majorities in both Houses—insisted on a closer involvement in such decisions.[54]

To reintroduce such outdated language, the report continued, would be counterproductive since it might convey the mistaken impression that Congress was once again prepared to sanction unilateral military initiatives on the part of the President. Turning to the case at hand, the committee emphasized that, regardless of U.S. policy vis-à-vis Cuba or any other country, "the President has a clear obligation under the War Powers

Act to consult with the Congress prior to any future decision to commit combat forces to El Salvador."[55]

The Symms Amendment failed in committee, but it gathered additional Senate support when the Reagan Administration, after some hesitation, agreed to support it publicly. On August 10, 1982, it was reintroduced as an amendment to the foreign assistance bill then pending. It passed the next day by a vote of 68 to 28. The Percy Amendment was then offered as a substitute but failed by a vote of 47 to 52.[56] The floor debate preceding these votes made it clear that a substantial majority of the Senate wished to go on record with a strong anti-Communist statement on Central America and that most Senators were not particularly concerned with the potential implications of such a statement on the war powers issue. Accordingly, Senators voted for the measure that was seen as strongest and that was supported by the President. Despite this setback, Senator Percy and others successfully amended the Symms resolution to specify that it did not constitute "specific statutory authorization" for the use of American armed forces in combat within the meaning of the WPR; there were only two dissenting votes (Senators Goldwater and John East [R-NC]).[57]

This amendment, and the ease with which it passed, seemed to demonstrate that general support for the WPR, at least at the theoretical level, subsisted in the Senate. The analogy to the quickly passed and later much regretted Tonkin Gulf Resolution, frequently drawn in the debate on the Symms Amendment, was not lost on the Senate; there was a clear understanding that the Senate did not intend to abandon future involvement in policymaking on the issues covered by the Symms Amendment because it had passed the legislation. On the other hand, the insistence of Senators Percy and Byrd on the need for an explicit disclaimer suggested that supporters of the WPR were sufficiently uncertain of its position as to worry that even a rhetorical exercise such as the Symms Amendment might result in its being circumvented.

In fact, this rather confused debate seems to mark the last serious attempt on the part of either House to apply the WPR directly to events in Central America. Although WPR-based measures were introduced in 1983, they were never formally considered in committee or acted upon on the floor of the House or Senate.[58] Not only did these attempts to apply the WPR to the situation in Central America garner little support in Congress, they do not seem to have made a significant impact on public opinion. It is not surprising, then, that Congress ignored the potentially marginal violations of the WPR reported in the following years and failed to mention the resolution in subsequent attempts to limit U.S. military activities in Central America.

On the surface, these brief rhetorical clashes over the applicability of the WPR to U.S. activities in El Salvador closely resembled the debates of the Ford and Carter Administrations. Following the pattern set in those cases, the Administration easily fended off attempts to apply the WPR to ambiguous situations, while Members of Congress proved unwilling to enact measures to strengthen the resolution. The difference in the case of El Salvador was that while the 1970s debates were triggered by events that were either very minor or largely noncontroversial, the question of war powers in 1981 and 1982 was part of a much broader political debate over the Reagan Administration's policy on Central America.

In this context, the WPR emerged as one of several of tools for Members of Congress who opposed the basic direction of the Administration's policies to use in pursuit of their ultimate goal—to reverse that policy. The WPR did not prove to be a particularly effective tool, however, as the Reagan Administration made good use of the means established by its predecessors to deflect all attempts to invoke the resolution.

At the same time, the Administration's congressional supporters refused to be distracted from achieving their policy goals by abstract considerations of the balance of power among the branches of the U.S. government. Insofar as the Republicans controlled the Senate, and the Democratic majority in the House was often divided when the President took a strong stand on an issue, this viewpoint went effectively unchallenged. Thus, in the early 1980s, the question of applying the WPR was caught up, and to a great extent lost, in the broader political debate over Central America.

U.S. Forces in Honduras

After 1983 the focus of public and congressional debate shifted from an almost exclusive interest in El Salvador to the wider issue of U.S. activities in the entire Central American region. While the presence of U.S.

advisors in El Salvador remained controversial, the issue lost much of its political immediacy after 1983, due in large part to the significant improvement of the Salvadoran political and human rights situation. Jose Napoleon Duarte's election as President of El Salvador, which was extremely well received in U.S. political circles, encouraged a more benevolent congressional attitude.

The Reagan Administration's stepped-up efforts to put pressure on the Sandinista regime in Nicaragua beginning in 1983 kept congressional attention focused on Central America. Directly relevant to the war powers question was the increasing U.S. military presence in Honduras, which was linked both to the situation in El Salvador and to efforts to contain Nicaragua and support the anti-Sandinista insurgents. From less than 100 in the years before 1983, the number of U.S military personnel in Honduras jumped to well over 1,000 in 1984 and subsequent years.

In the spring and summer of 1983, some 1,000 U.S. military personnel were deployed to a unit known as "Task Force Bravo," at Palmerola Air Force Base in Honduras, to coordinate U.S. military exercises in Honduras and U.S. assistance to the Honduran armed forces. From June 1983 to the summer of 1985, U.S. forces also operated a Regional Military Training Center in northern Honduras, where forces from El Salvador, as well as Honduras and Costa Rica, received training from U.S. personnel. While neither of these activities involved U.S. forces in hostilities, it seems reasonable to conclude that if the forces involved were "equipped for combat" this change in the number of U.S. personnel would qualify as a "significant increase" under the terms of Section 4(a)(3) of the WPR. Nonetheless, Members of Congress made little effort to pursue the question of WPR applicability in this case.

U.S. forces based in Honduras also engaged in combat support missions in both Honduras and El Salvador. In the spring of 1984, it was reported that U.S. pilots were flying tactical reconnaissance missions over El Salvador from Honduran bases in direct support of the Salvadoran Army. The U.S. ambassador in El Salvador eventually confirmed that these missions were being flown but asserted that since the aircraft in question were unarmed, the WPR was not applicable.[59] Congress did not pursue the question.

In March 1986 U.S. Army helicopters and crews transported Honduran troops to remote regions in response to incursions into Honduras by

Nicaraguan troops, presumably as a result of Nicaraguan operations against the anti-Sandinista insurgents based in Honduras. These activities could be interpreted as falling under the provisions of Section 8 of the WPR, which specifies that the participation by U.S. troops in the movement of foreign troops involved in hostilities constitutes the "introduction of U.S. armed forces." The Reagan Administration, however, avoided a serious debate on WPR compliance in both cases by assuring the Congress that the U.S. forces themselves were not involved in hostilities.[60]

Thus while the political and military implications of the U.S. military presence in Honduras were the subject of considerable debate, Congress made relatively little effort to apply the provisions of the WPR. Perhaps congressional leaders realized that the type of activities in question had already been conceded in principle over the course of past Administrations. Nevertheless, there was a considerable contrast between the Congress' reluctance even to discuss applying provisions of the WPR to U.S. activities in Honduras from 1983 onward, and its repeated, albeit unsuccessful, efforts to invoke the resolution with regard to U.S. activities in El Salvador in 1981 and 1982. Even though there were far more U.S. personnel in Honduras than in El Salvador, the failure of initiatives in the early years of the Reagan Administration apparently convinced the Congress that the war powers issue was not worth pursuing in the context of Central America.

Political factors within the two Houses of Congress also contributed to congressional inaction. In the Senate, the Republican majority had little interest in opposing the methods of the President's policy, the goals of which it generally supported, so long as the actual incidents involved were minor and did not generate significant public controversy. The House of Representatives, and in particular the Foreign Affairs Committee, had been more aggressive in pursuing this issue in 1981 and 1982. Both Speaker O'Neill and Chairman Zablocki publicly opposed Reagan Administration policy in Central America, although the President's popularity at the time, even among House Democrats, restrained drastic steps to oppose his policy. After 1983, however, these leaders chose to focus on the question of covert assistance to Nicaraguan insurgents, eclipsing the issue of U.S. forces in Honduras.

There was also a marked decline in the activism of the Foreign Affairs Committee on Central American issues after the death of Clement

Zablocki in 1983. The new chairman, Congressman Dante Fascell, had been one of the few prominent Democrats to support the Administration's policy in El Salvador in 1981 and 1982. After taking the chair, Fascell was somewhat more restrained by the House leadership's positions, but he certainly did not encourage the committee to undertake new initiatives to curtail the Administration's flexibility in Central America. The WPR, which was solely within the jurisdiction of the Foreign Affairs Committee, thus lost much of its usefulness as a means of expressing opposition to Administration policy in Central America.

PURSE-STRING RESTRICTIONS IN CENTRAL AMERICA

Developments in related areas of foreign policy support the conclusions about the Legislative-Executive balance of power drawn from the war powers debates of the Reagan Administration. This is particularly apparent in an examination of congressional attempts to influence the Reagan Administration's foreign policy initiatives by means of vehicles other than the WPR. The failure of congressional power of the purse to limit U.S. military activities in Central America parallels, in many ways, the ineffectual attempts to apply the WPR to events in El Salvador.

Given the disappointing results of the attempts to apply the WPR to Reagan Administration policy in El Salvador, as well as the less militant position on Central America taken by the Foreign Affairs Committee after 1983, Members of the House of Representatives wishing to reduce the level of the U.S. military presence in Central America turned increasingly to other legislative tactics, and thus to different committees. In particular, attempts were made in the Appropriations and Armed Services Committees to impose ad hoc limits on funding for specific activities.

Military Exercises in Honduras

The Reagan Administration's most visible militaray activities in Central America took the form of a series of military exercises of unprecedented scope and duration held in Honduras beginning in 1983. Although the Administration presented these maneuvers as routine training exercises, a number of observers in and out of Congress concluded that the operations were a pretext to justify the establishment of a long-term military presence in Central America. Indeed, the Administration made no secret of the fact that the exercises provided a means of putting political and military pressure on the government of Nicaragua.

These exercises involved up to 6,000 U.S. troops in a variety of activities such as amphibious landings, naval patrols, and counterinsurgency operations. Taken together, they accounted for the virtually uninterrupted presence of U.S. combat forces in Honduras from early 1983 onward. While no hostilities ensued, the U.S. forces involved were certainly "equipped for combat," and the scale and duration of the U.S. military presence suggested that it might be interpreted as a "significant increase" in U.S. forces in Honduras, thus subject to the terms of Section 4(a)(3) of the WPR.

Lending further credence to the claim that the exercises were in fact a pretext for a permanently enlarged U.S. presence in Honduras was the fact that they involved the construction of permanent military facilities. Beginning in 1983, U.S. forces built or upgraded at least seven Honduran military airfields, as well as two radar surveillance posts. Other engineering work, such as the construction of roads and antitank defenses were also undertaken.[61]

Opponents of the Administration's policy sought to cut off funding for these projects. Since the President's position found strong and consistent support among the Senate's Republican majority, the political maneuvering fell into a pattern closely resembling that of House-Senate-Administration negotiations over controversial military procurement questions during 1981–1986. Administration requests were usually granted by the Senate and opposed in the House. Eventually, a legislative compromise provided a smaller sum than that requested by the Administration and in some cases incorporated reporting requirements and minor restrictions. In no case was an activity prohibited altogether.

The Reagan Administration requested $21 million in fiscal year 1983 to improve three airfields in Honduras. While attempts to delete the entire request failed, the final authorization provided $13 million for only two of the projected sites.[62] In addition, the House Armed Services Committee report accompanying the Military Construction Authorization Bill urged the Administration to "proceed with extreme caution so as not to exacerbate the problems already existing in this part of the world."[63]

The FY 1984 request for $8 million to improve one site not funded in 1983 was approved with the restriction that the funds not be obligated until the Administration provided a statement of its ultimate construction plans for the region. In making this stipulation, the House Appropriations Committee noted that it was "concerned . . . with increased tensions in Central America and intends to monitor all military construction in that area very carefully."[64] Although the funds were ultimately appropriated, along with an additional $8.7 million for FY 1985, the committee noted that it "questioned the long-term accuracy" of the Administration's reports.[65]

In addition, it became known that operational funds had been employed to construct so-called temporary facilities in the course of military exercises that in fact remained in use after the official termination of those exercises. Operations and maintenance funds are appropriated as a yearly lump sum covering a specific aspect of military activity, not in discrete amounts for individual projects; this usage had thus deprived Congress of detailed financial oversight. Since operational funds are permitted only for temporary construction, the relative permanence of the facilities in question was key. A 1984 General Accounting Office report noting this development concluded that such projects were "less temporary" than certain others that, in the past, had been defined as permanent. Accordingly, funding them from operations and maintenance appropriations was inappropriate.[66]

In an effort to regain a measure of control over activities in Central America, Congress included a provision in the continuing resolution for FY 1985, passed in October 1984 (P.L. 98-473, Section 101), requiring that the Secretary of Defense give prior notice to the Appropriations and Armed Services Committees of the plans and scope of any proposed military exercises involving U.S. personnel if amounts to be expended for construction, either temporary or permanent, would exceed $100,000.

Despite these efforts, the Administration's plans for military activities in Honduras were not seriously hampered. Press reports in 1986 indicated that as many as nine airfields were constructed or improved significantly over the course of exercises in the previous year.[67] Nor were the Administration's plans for the future scaled down. In a report submitted to the House and Senate Appropriations Committees in February 1986, the Defense Department stated that it planned to request some $29.8 million for military construction projects in Honduras in the fiscal years 1986 through 1990, in addition to unspecified amounts of operational funding.[68] On the whole, it seems that while U.S. military policy in Central America received a certain amount of congressional attention, the Administration's persistence, together with the discipline of the Republican majority in the Senate, ensured that planned activities in Honduras were carried out. Administration programs were slowed and, to a certain extent, limited, but never cancelled or even seriously restricted.

The Foley Amendment

The power of the political alliance between the President and Senate Republicans was demonstrated anew when House Members attempted to attach broad prior restraints on the President's options in Central America to spending bills. These attempts parallel the Byrd Amendment as the fiscal tactics detailed above paralleled attempts to invoke the WPR with regard to El Salvador. By employing Congress' power of the purse, Members sought to circumvent the problems that had thwarted attempts to apply the WPR, not the least of which was the position taken by Chairman Fascell and the House Foreign Affairs Committee. No constitutional or procedural problems stood in the way of these efforts in the House; the political balance of power in the early 1980s, however, virtually ensured their failure in the Senate.

In the best known example of this tactic, Thomas Foley (D-WA), the Majority Whip of the House, introduced an amendment to the FY 1985 Defense Authorization Bill (H.R. 1872, 98th Cong.) that would have barred the introduction of U.S. troops into El Salvador or Nicaragua for combat without prior congressional authorization except in cases of clear threats to the security of U.S. military or diplomatic personnel or of the United States itself. Significantly, the authors of this measure, presumably having learned from the experience of the WPR, took care to define "combat" within the legislation itself as "the introduction of United States armed forces for the purpose of delivering weapons fire against an enemy."[69]

Despite spirited opposition from the Republican minority—most of which came after the amendment had been approved by a roll call vote of 341 to 64—attempts to weaken the amendment were turned aside. The strongest of these, proposed by Congressman Duncan Hunter (R-CA), would have waived the provisions of the Foley Amendment if the President determined that "there existed a Soviet, Soviet-bloc, Cuban, or other Communist threat to the region." Since President Reagan and his advisors had made precisely that claim throughout his Presidency, this amounted to a de facto annulment of the prohibition on the use of U.S. forces in combat. Hunter's amendment was rejected by a vote of 288 to 99. The only amendment that passed was one proposed by Congressman Caroll Campbell, Jr. (R-SC) that extended Foley's provisions to all of Central America but stipulated that the legislation in no way lessened the President's power as commander-in-chief. Since Foley and his allies had maintained from the start that it was not their intention to diminish the President's legitimate constitutional powers, they did not oppose this amendment, which passed by a voice vote.

Not surprisingly, a different fate awaited the Foley Amendment in the Senate. Introduced by Senators Edward Kennedy (D-MA) and Mark Hatfield (R-OR), the measure failed by 63 votes to 31. A similar measure that dealt only with El Salvador, introduced as an amendment to an "urgent supplemental appropriation" bill by Senator Patrick Leahy (D-VT), had been defeated by a vote of 59 to 36 a month earlier.[70] In effect, the fate of these measures paralleled that of the earlier Byrd Amendment. Proposed as amendments to money bills instead of to the WPR, they bypassed the Foreign Relations Committee, but their defeat on the floor was virtually assured. Nevertheless, the strong support for language of this sort demonstrated in the House enabled proponents of the Foley Amendment to win at least a symbolic compromise at the time of the House-Senate Conference on the Defense Authorization Bill. In the end, Foley's language was retained as a non-binding sense-of-the-Congress provision of the Defense Authorization Act for FY 1985 (P.L. 98-525, Section 310). Similar nonbinding language was also included in the FY 1986 Defense Authorization Bill.

Conclusion

In determining the outcome of the debate over military activities in Central America, the intra-congressional balance of power was at least as important as the Executive-Legislative balance. Thus a more united Congress might be able to utilize its power of the purse to attain a narrow war powers objective. If House and Senate were to agree to omit funding for a specific activity and provide safeguards to ensure that funds appropriated for other purposes were not transferred, the President would have few viable options.

The legislative tactics employed by the House majority are not automatically doomed to failure when the President's allies control one of the Houses of Congress; success does, however, require exceptional circumstances. In order to cut off funding for military construction in Honduras or secure passage of the Foley Amendment, the House would have had to defeat not only the President but also the Senate by holding the entire Defense Authorization Bill—and perhaps the appropriation bill as well—hostage to this provision.

When dealing with politically sensitive issues, this extreme tactic can sometimes succeed. Even in such circumstances, however, the multiple opportunities that the congressional appropriations process provides to reinsert previously deleted funding make cutoffs difficult at best. In this case, moreover, the relative lack of public controversy surrounding the projects in question—indeed of public awareness of their existence in the absence of major events—left opponents with very little political leverage; in the end, enough House Democrats voted for compromise proposals to ensure continuation of the Administration's projects in Honduras.

THE POWER OF PERSUASION

Two general observations emerge from the various clashes over the Reagan Administration's Central American policy; both reinforce the conclusions reached concerning military initiatives in Grenada and Libya.

First, the Administration seemed to understand and observe practical limits on acceptable U.S. military activity. In the cases of Grenada and Libya, the crucial variable was time—so long as operations were brief, the President could expect little effective opposition. In Central America, where long-term involvement was key to the Administration's plans, the principal factor was the U.S. forces' low profile—in particular, the absence of unambiguous involvement in combat. By carefully remaining within these limits, the Reagan Administration headed off all attempts to invoke the WPR, even in circumstances where a good technical case might have been made for its applicability. In so doing, however, the Administration implicitly accepted significant limitations on its freedom of action.

Second, even when the policy in question was quite controversial, the WPR remained essentially ineffective in the absence of congressional unity. Members who supported the President politically showed repeatedly that they were unwilling to deviate from that support in order to defend the institutional prerogatives of the Congress in potentially ambiguous situations—although they remained willing to reaffirm those prerogatives in theory, as demonstrated by the outcome of the debate on the Symms Amendment. As a weapon in congressional "guerrilla fighting," the WPR served only to provoke debate; it did not allow even a determined minority actually to change policy.

The fate of the Foley Amendment, however, demonstrated that the larger outcome of the debate on Central American policy was primarily due not to the shortcomings of the WPR but rather to the general balance of political power, both between Congress and the President and within the Legislative branch. While the continuation of funding for U.S. military activities in Honduras was undeniably a victory for the President and a political setback for certain Members of Congress, it was not an institutional defeat for the Congress as a whole. This distinction is critical. The ability to persuade Members of Congress—even those of the opposing party—is, after all, one of the legitimate qualities of successful Presidents. The test of Congress' institutional power comes when this persuasion fails.

5 CONGRESS DEFENDS ITS GAINS

If the political success of the Reagan Administration's policy in Libya, Grenada, and Central America illustrated the extent of the President's freedom of action, the events and controversy that arose from the Administration's initiatives in Lebanon and Nicaragua confirmed that the Congress would react strongly if the President's actions exceeded the implicit boundaries established by the precedents of the 1970s. These cases, accordingly, are of the highest significance in determining the nature of the institutional balance of power in the 1980s. Although very different in circumstances and outcome, each in its own way demonstrates the changes that have occurred since the pre-Vietnam War days of unquestioned presidential supremacy.

U.S. PARTICIPATION IN THE BEIRUT MULTINATIONAL FORCE

The presence of U.S. Marines in Beirut, the only case since the end of the Vietnam War in which U.S. troops participated in a hostile situation over an extended period of time, has unique significance in the context of the war powers debate. Out of this incident came the first formal legislation implementing the key operative sections of the WPR in a real-world situation. Moreover, the use made of the WPR in this situation provided a hopeful sign that the resolution might serve as a means of compromise and accommodation between the Legislative and Executive branches rather than a point of confrontation.

Background

The situation that led to the U.S. intervention in Lebanon as part of the three-nation multinational force (MNF) in Beirut had its roots in the 1982 Israeli invasion of southern Lebanon, which resulted in the concentration of a large number of Palestine Liberation Organization (PLO) fighters in western Beirut. International efforts followed to negotiate a truce during which these fighters could be evacuated from Beirut, sparing the city further destruction and bloodshed.

On August 20, 1982, Israel, the PLO, and the government of Lebanon reached an agreement under the terms of which PLO forces would be evacuated from West Beirut. The Lebanese government agreed to ensure security for the operation with the assistance of a 2,100-man force of troops from France, Italy, and the United States.[1] The MNF went into Beirut on August 24, carried out the evacuation smoothly, and left the city on September 10.[2]

In the following days, however, several violent events in Beirut indicated that the fragile Lebanese government was on the brink of total collapse. On September 14, Bashir Gemayel, Lebanon's newly elected President, was assassinated. On the next day, Israeli forces moved forward to occupy all of Beirut. Finally, on September 18 and 19, Palestinian civilians in refugee camps outside of Beirut were massacred by members of a pro-Israeli Lebanese militia.[3] Faced with this desperate situation, the Lebanese government requested that the MNF be redeployed to Beirut; the troops consequently returned on September 20. President Reagan announced that U.S. troops would be in Beirut for a "limited period of time" and that their mission would be confined to "enabling the Lebanese government to resume full sovereignty over its capital." At a press conference the following week, however, the President suggested a much broader role for the MNF, stating that the marines would not be withdrawn until all foreign forces were out of Lebanon.[4]

Optimistic as this objective was, given the long history of foreign military presence in Lebanon, it was arguably not unrealizable at the time. Indeed, U.S.-mediated negotiations among the various Lebanese factions and between the coalition government of Lebanon and Israel seemed to be making progress, and an agreement was reached between the Lebanese and Israeli governments on May 17, 1983. Under this treaty, Israel agreed to withdraw its forces from Lebanon, although retaining the possibility of engaging in "security" operations in the southern part of the country. The Lebanese government, in turn, agreed to normalize its relationship with Israel. The accord implied the withdrawal of Syrian forces that had controlled a large portion of Lebanon since 1976, when they had been called in as a peacekeeping force during the Lebanese civil war.[5] How this was to be accomplished, though, was far from apparent.

Indeed, far from serving as the first step in a more general settlement of the Lebanese conflict, the U.S.-sponsored agreement proved an impediment to further progress. The government of Syria, which had not been a party to the negotiations, denounced the treaty even before its official signature and made clear that it had no intention of withdrawing its forces from Lebanon or of cooperating with any aspect of the U.S.-sponsored peace plan.[6] As a result, pro-Syrian factions within Lebanon dropped all pretense of cooperating with the central government, and the level of violence in Beirut and throughout Lebanon escalated once again. By the summer of 1983, heavy fighting was underway in a number of locations in and around the Lebanese capital.

This renewed outbreak of sectarian violence dramatically illustrated the failure of attempts by the U.S. and Lebanese leaders to reconstitute the government of Lebanon and, in particular, the Lebanese Armed Forces (LAF) as truly "national" institutions, representative of the Lebanese population as a whole and whose authority would be accepted by all factions. Instead, the LAF was increasingly split down religious and political grounds; the Christian-dominated units that remained actively loyal to the government were reduced once again to their pre-1982 status—one faction among many, and by no means the strongest militarily. In this context, cooperation between the LAF and the MNF took on a very different significance for the Lebanese than had been intended. Rather than a neutral force working for national reconciliation and unity, the MNF was perceived as the military ally of one of the belligerent forces. The United States had been particularly generous in its military support to the government of Lebanon and the LAF. Accordingly, the government's opponents considered U.S. forces in Beirut to be legitimate targets.

Thus the MNF forces came under sustained rocket and artillery fire for the first time since their arrival. The first U.S. casualty occurred on August 29, 1983,[7] and more followed in the next weeks. U.S. forces responded to the attacks with naval gunfire from U.S. ships off shore. Although taken in self-defense, this action represented a further escalation of the U.S. role in the Lebanese conflict and one more step away from the original peacekeeping role of the MNF. For the remainder of their stay in Lebanon, U.S. forces would be forced to devote most of their efforts to self-protection.

The marines' perceived role as ally of the embattled LAF was reinforced in September 1983, when Israeli forces were withdrawn from positions in the Chouf Mountains overlooking Beirut. When the efforts of the LAF to occupy this strategic position were met with stiff resistance from the militia forces, gunfire from U.S. ships was employed in direct support of LAF operations. Although U.S. military and government spokesmen portrayed this action as nothing more than self-defense on the part of U.S. forces—who, the spokesmen asserted, would be in danger if the positions overlooking their compound were occupied by hostile forces—it was interpreted in Lebanon as a further token of a military alliance between the U.S. forces and the Lebanese army.[8]

Attacks on the marine contingent increased in the following weeks, culminating in the October 23 detonation of a suicide truck-bomb outside of marine headquarters that killed 241 individuals. In retaliation for this attack, which was generally believed to have been carried out by Syrian-backed forces, U.S. carrier-based aircraft flew reconnaissance and then attack missions over Syrian-controlled areas of Lebanon during the fall and winter of 1983–84. The marines in Beirut continued to receive and return artillery and small arms fire, suffering additional casualties throughout this period. On February 7, 1984, President Reagan announced that the marines would be redeployed to offshore ships.[9] U.S. naval forces remained in position off the coast of Lebanon for some weeks thereafter and continued to provide gunfire and air support for the Lebanese army. President Reagan officially informed the Congress of the end of U.S. participation in the MNF on March 31, 1984, with letters to the Speaker and President Pro Tem.

Congressional interest in the role played by U.S. troops in Lebanon was intense throughout the duration of the two MNF deployments. Three episodes are of particular interest as war powers issues. The first is the initial deployment of U.S. forces, which prompted questions about the adequacy of Executive-Legislative consultation and the need for congressional authorization of the deployment. The most widely known congressional action concerning Lebanon was the passage of the Multi-National Force in Lebanon Resolution (MFLR), which took place over a year after the marines were first deployed to Beirut. The political debates and negotiations that preceeded this legislation are the best example to date of the WPR's potential as a vehicle for compromise between the branches of government. The significance and wisdom of the MFLR, as well as its impact on the larger issue of war powers, remain controversial, however. Finally, Congress played an important, if indirect, role in influencing President Reagan's eventual decision to withdraw U.S. forces from Lebanon.

Congress and the Deployment of U.S. Forces

The issues surrounding the initial deployment of U.S. Marines to Lebanon echoed those of other post-1973 war powers situations—adequacy of consultation and the technicalities of reporting. Most participants agree that the President did involve congressional leaders in timely consultation before deployment of the first MNF. The disagreements that arose from these interchanges, however, were resolved by unilateral presidential decisions rather than by Executive-Legislative consensus.

Since there was no doubt that the forces in Lebanon would be "equipped for combat," the point at issue became the question of whether they would be exposed to actual or imminent hostilities. As on previous occasions, the Executive branch was extremely reluctant to apply Section 4(a)(1) of the WPR. Accordingly, President Reagan sought to rule out the possibility that U.S. forces would be exposed to hostilities when he announced on July 6 that he had agreed in principle to the MNF plan then being negotiated. While the President pledged to comply with the WPR, however, he did not refer to a specific section or provision of the resolution. Meeting with a bipartisan group of congressional leaders on July 13, President Reagan added that the use of U.S. troops, if any, would be "for a very short period."[10]

Congressional response to these statements was guarded. Chairman Zablocki informed the President that in the contingency he had described, Section 4(a)(1) of the WPR would apply and should be cited explicitly. Zablocki characterized attempts to circumvent Section 4(a)(1) as "capricious" and as having "incalculable effects on Executive-Legislative relations on a variety of foreign policy issues."[11]

Senator Charles Percy (R-IL), the Republican chairman of the Senate Foreign Relations Committee, gave his tentative approval to the President's plan if the safety of the U.S. troops could be guaranteed and if Israel pledged not to move troops into West Beirut or otherwise to interfere with the MNF. Even in these circumstances, however, Percy maintained that in his opinion Section 4(a)(1) would apply.[12] Senate Majority Leader Howard Baker (R-TN) was even less favorable toward using U.S. troops in Beirut, stating that he had alerted the President to his opposition to such a move but reserved the right to change his mind.[13]

The agreement announced on August 20 seemed to meet the criteria set by the President and congressional leaders. All parties in Beirut agreed to a cease-fire, and the Israeli government pledged to keep its forces out of West Beirut. In his report to Congress following the August 24 deployment of U.S. forces, moreover, the President stated that U.S. forces were in Beirut on a "limited and temporary basis" and would not undertake combat responsibilities.[14] State Department spokesmen later specified that the marines would not be deployed for longer than thirty days.

President Reagan's report, while submitted "pursuant to the WPR," did not cite Section 4(a)(1). Instead, the President followed the questionable precedent of previous Administrations—counter to his own Administration's precedent set the previous year on the occasion of the deployment of U.S. forces to the Sinai—citing no particular section in his report. As before, no effective congressional protest was made on this point.

While the President's contention that U.S. forces would not be exposed to hostilities was borne out, a strong case could be made that the tense situation in the Lebanese capital, coupled with the large number of heavily armed and notoriously ill-disciplined forces on the scene, comprised a condition of imminent hostilities as understood by the authors of the WPR. Such definitional ambiguities, however, had been settled to the Executive's advantage in the 1970s, and President Reagan would be unlikely to rescind that advantage. In any case, the perceived success of the MNF's mission ensured that no serious challenges to the President's methods would be made.

As it happened, however, the Administration used the congressional approval of the first MNF to justify the deployment of U.S. forces with the second MNF without additional consultation with Congress. The use of this second force, however, with its vaguely defined and open-ended mission, was a very different proposition from that of the first; given the President's broad objectives, a gradual increase in the role of U.S. forces in Beirut, and perhaps throughout Lebanon, could not be ruled out. This difference, however, did not lead to additional consultation, nor was it reflected in the President's second report to Congress.

President Reagan's September 29, 1982 report announcing U.S. participation in the second MNF was patterned after the first, avoiding any overt reference to Section 4(a)(1) of the WPR and downplaying the possibility that U.S. forces might be exposed to combat. Nevertheless, Senators Claiborne Pell (D-RI) and Percy, in a joint letter to President Reagan, expressed their opinion that Section 4(a)(1) was applicable. Percy went so far as to assert that the sixty-day clock would apply whether or not the President formally invoked Section 4(a)(1), implying that congressional authorization would be required within sixty days if U.S. troops were to remain in Lebanon.[16] The Administration sought no such authorization, however, and Congress made no attempt to force the withdrawal of the U.S. troops after sixty days had passed.

The relative calm and the optimistic political situation that characterized the first several months of the MNF's stay in Beirut did much to silence potential critics. In June 1983, following the announcement of the Israeli-Lebanese accord, Congress passed and the President signed the Lebanon Emergency Assistance Act (LEAA), which, in addition to providing large-scale U.S. economic and military aid to the government of

Lebanon, confirmed the role of U.S. forces in the MNF for an indefinite period of time. Members of Congress attempted to place limits on the President's use of U.S. forces, asserting that

> the President shall obtain statutory authorization from the Congress with regard to any substantial expansion in the number or role in Lebanon of United States Armed Forces, including the introduction of United States Armed Forces into Lebanon in conjunction with agreements providing for the withdrawal of all foreign troops from Lebanon and for the creation of a new multinational peacekeeping force in Lebanon.[16]

Section 4(b) of the LEAA also noted that the Act would not modify, limit, or supersede the provisions of the WPR.

With the passage of the LEAA, Congress went on record unequivocally as supporting the presence and the stated goals of U.S. participation in the MNF for an indefinite period of time. Shortly thereafter, however, the changing situation in Lebanon would work a remarkable change in congressional attitudes.

The Multinational Force in Lebanon Resolution

Over the course of the summer of 1983, a number of questions were raised as to whether the Administration was in fact complying with the terms of the LEAA. During that time, the U.S. force was reportedly increased by at least 600 men, a significant number when added to a force that numbered only 1,200. More serious was the question of whether the role of the marines had changed significantly and irrevocably after U.S. artillery became actively involved in providing support for Lebanese government forces.[17] In the absence of significant public controversy, however, these "technical" issues lacked political immediacy, and Congress did not pursue them aggressively.

Congress' interest in reexamining the role of the MNF heightened after the U.S. forces began to suffer casualties. Even then, however, the leaders of both Houses were not eager to challenge the President directly. Instead, responding to the increasing level of violence in Beirut, Members who had opposed U.S. participation in the MNF from the outset called for the immediate withdrawal of U.S forces. This sentiment took legislative form on September 21, when the House Appropriations Committee accepted an amendment to a continuing resolution then pending proposed by Congressman Clarence Long (D-MD), chairman of the Foreign Operations Appropriations Subcommittee, to cut off all funds for U.S. forces in Lebanon on December 1 unless the President reported to the Congress under the terms of Section 4(a)(1).

Long's proposal echoed the sentiments of a growing number of Members who were frustrated by the President's rigidity and by the unwillingness of congressional foreign policy leaders to confront the Administration. Given the record of executive hostility to Section 4(a)(1), the reference to the WPR in Long's amendment was chiefly rhetorical; Long and his allies sought to legislate foreign policy directly through the appropriations process. This was a return to the legislative tactics of the early 1970s when purse-string amendments from the floor had short-circuited the established policy process. In the very different political environment of the 1980s, however, this tactic could not work. The leadership's control over the House was much stronger and, in any case, the Republican-controlled Senate stood as an insurmountable obstacle to such an open repudiation of the President's policy.

The political strength of Long's stance was that it could intensify and focus the public debate on the Administration's Lebanon policy, placing the President and the House leadership in a difficult position. While the Administration's position in Congress seemed secure, at least in the short term, support for its policy among the electorate at large was declining as the level of violence—and the number of U.S. casualties—increased. Unless the U.S. commitment could be vindicated by a spectacular diplomatic breakthrough (an increasingly slim hope by late 1983), the President and his allies would be left defending an unpopular, costly, and seemingly open-ended military commitment going into an election year. In these circumstances, attacks such as Long's could do considerable damage. The House leadership, meanwhile, risked losing political credibility if it allowed itself to be identified solely with the President's position. Out of this uncomfortable situation arose an unlikely coalition consisting of the President, the House Democratic leadership, and Senate Republicans. All three had a strong interest in forging a broadly acceptable compromise on this issue, which would defuse its political explosiveness. The WPR offered a means for accomplishing their goal.

By this time, the WPR itself was very much in question. On August 30, 1983, the President had submitted a report to Congress that noted the deaths of two U.S. Marines in Beirut and cited Section 4 of the WPR. Nowhere did it indicate, however, that the Administration recognized the applicability of Section 4(a)(1) in this case. Yet even by previous Administrations' definitions the situation of the U.S. forces in Lebanon in the autumn of 1983 was obviously one of "hostilities." In the words of Senator Percy, "We have people up there in helicopters, we're shooting rockets and artillery—If that's not imminent hostilities, I don't know what is." Failure to apply the WPR to its full extent would effectively signify its demise as a useful policy instrument: "If the WPR is not invoked," asserted Senator Lloyd Bentsen (D-TX), "it is worthless, it is a scrap of paper and we ought to throw it away."[18] Republican Members of Congress still refused to challenge the Administration directly, however, and attempts by Senate Democrats to introduce legislation invoking the WPR progressed no further than the Foreign Relations Committee.

While Chairman Percy and Senate Majority Leader Howard Baker agreed with their Democratic colleagues that the WPR should be invoked, they were not prepared to do so in defiance of the President; instead, they sought to include an invocation in a larger compromise. A period of intensive negotiation with the White House followed. In the end, the Republican Senators, with the strong backing of Speaker O'Neill, convinced the President and his advisors that the Administration must make at least a symbolic acquiescence to the provisions of the WPR if a major political confrontation were to be avoided.

The Multinational Force in Lebanon Resolution (MFLR) (P.L. 98-119), which emerged from the negotiations, recognized that "significant hostilities" under the terms of the WPR were indeed underway in Beirut, and that Section 4(a)(1) had gone into effect on August 29, the date of the first U.S. casualties.[19] Thereupon, the MFLR authorized the President to maintain U.S. forces in Lebanon for eighteen months from the date of the legislation's implementation, unless Congress chose to extend the deadline. The forces could be withdrawn in less than eighteen months if the President deemed it appropriate or if Congress passed a Joint Resolution to that effect. While U.S. forces remained in Lebanon, the President was required to submit a report to Congress every three months detailing their status, composition, and activities, as well as the progress being made toward national reconciliation in Lebanon. The report was also to explain how continued deployment of U.S. forces in Lebanon furthered the U.S. national interest.

The MFLR further stipulated that U.S. forces were not to engage in any activities other than those specified in the 1982 agreement establishing the MNF, with the exception of actions taken in self-defense. Since the MFLR was written during an escalation of U.S. activities including naval gunfire and direct support of the LAF—all of which had publicly been justified as self-defense—and does not imply that these activities might have been inappropriate, many observers concluded that the latter provision could be interpreted quite broadly, perhaps to the extent of effectively superseding the former. Moreover, while the MFLR referred to the conditions set out in the LEAA, it did not imply that previous activities by U.S. forces had been improper under the terms of the earlier act—a belief held by many Members of Congress.

For this reason and others, the MFLR generated considerable controversy among both Members of Congress and other observers of the war powers debate. Most of the criticism came from liberals who believed that the Congress had given away too much. This point of view was articulated with particular force by Senate Democrats who, having been largely shut out of the negotiations that produced the MFLR, were not inclined to support it.

In the Minority Views appended to the Senate Foreign Relations Committee's report on the MFLR, Democratic senators defined three areas of disagreement:

> In our Judgment [the MFLR's] enactment would constitute (1) a dereliction of Congressional responsibility to uphold the principles and procedures of the War Powers Resolution of 1973; (2) a failure to require of the Administration a clearly articulated and persuasive statement of the missions which U.S. Marines have been deployed in Lebanon to implement; and (3) an 18 month "blank check" under which the Administration could pursue hitherto unspecified military objectives in Lebanon while asserting that it is operating under Congressional sanction.[20]

The first and third of these points have direct bearing on the question of war powers.

In defense of their first assertion, Democratic Members pointed out that Congress could have avoided ambiguity by simply passing a resolution triggering Section 4(a)(1) and reserving judgment on whether to authorize further U.S. activities in Lebanon until the President acknowledged that congressional authorization was, in fact, required. By combining the two steps into a single piece of legislation, however, the President was once again allowed to evade the question of whether he would ultimately be bound by the WPR's sixty-day limit.[21]

Indeed, statements by Administration spokesmen, in particular Secretary Shultz, left considerable doubt as to whether the President considered even the MFLR, which he proposed to sign, as an absolute limit on his power as commander-in-chief. In response to questions from Senator Paul Sarbanes (D-MD) in the course of Senate hearings on the MFLR, Shultz suggested that ". . . the President, or perhaps any of you if you were President . . . would be very reluctant to tie your hands and say that you could only order U.S. forces to do something after you [sic] had authorized it.[22]

In the days that followed, President Reagan attempted to reassure Congress of his goodwill. In a letter to Congress on September 27 he wrote:

> It would be my intention to seek Congressional authorization—as contemplated by the LEAA—if circumstances require any substantial expansion in the number or role of U.S. armed forces in Lebanon . . . I can assure you that if forces are needed in Lebanon beyond the 18 month period, it would be my intention to work together with the Congress with a view to taking action on mutually acceptable terms.[23]

Statements such as this, however, left unanswered the larger question of the President's legal responsibilities. While promising to "work together with the Congress," the President did not imply that he would consider himself bound by congressional decisions. Accordingly, his assurances did little to convert Members opposed to the MFLR.

Another controversial issue was the length of time for which the U.S. presence in Lebanon was authorized. A number of Members in both Houses considered eighteen months to be much too long. An attempt to shorten the period to six months was made in the Senate Foreign Relations Committee but failed by a single vote; similarly unsuccessful attempts were made by liberal House Members.

Members opposed to the MFLR also pointed out that the Administration's statements inspired little confidence that the President would feel obligated to withdraw U.S. forces in accordance with the eighteen-month or any other legislated deadline. To redress this potential ambiguity, Congressman Ted Weiss (D-NY) proposed that the House Foreign Affairs Committee amend the MFLR to cut off funding for U.S. forces in Lebanon at the end of the authorized period, thus ensuring Administration compliance.[24]

Chairman Clement Zablocki, who supported the position of the House leadership, strongly opposed this amendment. Significantly, Zablocki did not speak in opposition to the intent of Weiss' proposal. Rather, he claimed that the amendment would lead to the "unravelling" of the compromise reached with the President and to the demise of the entire MFLR. Congressman Steven Solarz (D-NY) added that, in any case, Congress could vote to cut off funds at some later date should this became necessary. It would be counterproductive, therefore, to include a "sure-veto" measure in the MFLR.[25]

In general, key moderate Democrats in the House such as Solarz and Lee Hamilton (D-IN), who were known as strong supporters of the WPR and who had previously argued for amendments to strengthen it, put forth considerable effort in support of the MFLR, defending it against liberal critics who saw the considerable freedom of action it left to the President as a betrayal of the spirit of the WPR. Solarz and his colleagues deemed it absolutely essential to reaffirm the WPR in this case—even at the cost of giving the President virtually a free hand for eighteen additional months.[26]

In the end, the fate of the MFLR in Congress rested largely with the coalition that had originally negotiated its terms. Republican leaders in the Senate persuaded all of their colleagues—even those such as Senator Goldwater who had serious reservations concerning the wisdom and constitutionality of the WPR itself—to vote for the MFLR, while Democrats remained in opposition. Although there was considerable debate dominated by the resolution's opponents, both in the Foreign Relations Committee and on the floor of the Senate, almost all votes split down strict party lines; the narrow but disciplined Republican majority carried the day.

The Democratic leadership in the House, particularly Speaker O'Neill and Chairman Zablocki, strongly supported the MFLR, having shaped it in negotiations with the President. House Republicans, by and large, favored the resolution out of a general sense of support for the President and, more urgently, in order to ensure that more radical legislation would be headed off. A substantial number of liberal Democrats rejected the compromise reached by the leadership and insisted on much stricter controls over U.S. activities in Lebanon, or on outright withdrawal of U.S. forces. Leading this group were Congressmen Long and David Obey (D-WI), who insisted that the President should be required to submit a report under Section 4(a)(1) and that purse-string restrictions be attached to any legislative authorization of further U.S. participation in the MNF.

Despite approval of the MFLR by the Foreign Affairs Committee with only two dissenting votes, the House leadership was concerned that amendments from the floor might attach provisions unacceptable to the President, such as a reduction of the authorized period from eighteen to six months. Accordingly, an unusually forceful exercise of the Speaker's power secured the resolution's final House passage. Debate was limited to four hours, no amendments were allowed, and only one alternative—the Long-Obey proposal—was permitted to reach the floor. As foreseen by the leadership, moderate Democrats who might have supported individual amendments were not prepared to vote for this complex and clearly confrontational alternative. In the end, the MFLR passed by a vote of 270 to 161.[27]

As promised, the President signed the MFLR into law on October 12, 1983. In his signing message, however, he pointed out that this action did not imply that the Executive branch accepted the constitutionality of the WPR:

> [Signing of the MFLR] should not be viewed as any acknowledgment that the President's constitutional authority can be impermissibly infringed by statute, that Congressional authorization would be required if and when the period specified in Section 5(b) of the WPR might be deemed to have [been] triggered and the period expired or that Section 6 of the MFLR may be interpreted to revise the President's constitutional authority to deploy United States Armed Forces.[28]

With this statement, President Reagan reasserted the theoretical position held by Richard Nixon and his successors. The fact remains, however, that the practical precedent set in this instance was one of negotiation and compromise by the President, as well by as the Congress. In the words of Senator Percy:

> We cannot legislatively prohibit the President from having reservations about the WPR. But we can collectively reaffirm its validity and thereby assure that the next time around we will have a less difficult time reaffirming the clear intent of the Constitution.[29]

A Positive Role for the WPR

Despite its limitations and shortcomings, the MFLR is the most successful attempt to date on the part of the Congress to influence the Executive branch through the WPR. More important, it is significant that in a situation with a high potential for confrontation, the WPR emerged as the vehicle for compromise. This fact stands as a powerful refutation to the arguments of those who claimed that the resolution's very existence would catalyze confrontation.

It also suggests that the authors of the WPR had correctly perceived the need for a statutory framework to exercise the collective judgment of Congress and the President in difficult foreign policy situations. The mechanisms of the WPR provided both a focus for debate and a model for structuring an Executive-Legislative agreement. At a time when the political need for a broad compromise was imperative, both sides saw the advantage of withholding constitutional and technical reservations in the interest of avoiding a mutually damaging confrontation.

A strong case can be made for the assertion that using the WPR as a flexible means for compromise and accommodation was precisely what its principal authors had intended when drafting the resolution in 1973. This is certainly true for Zablocki, whose support for the MFLR was unequivocal. In one of his final public appearances, Jacob Javits also expressed definite, albeit qualified, support for the MFLR. Interestingly, Javits' principal reservation concerned an aspect of the MFLR that had not generated much controversy—the use of a joint rather than a concurrent resolution as the potential vehicle for congressional termination of U.S. participation in the MNF. On balance, Javits concluded, the Administration and the Congress have each gained a major point in the proposed compromise on the War Powers Resolution. Congress has established that it may set the clock running under the resolution even if the President does not trigger it by giving appropriate notice under the proper sections of the resolution. . . . The President has gained the point that for the situation in Lebanon, the authority Congress gives him to continue their involvement must be by joint, not concurrent, resolution, thereby requiring the President's signature. The compromise avoids a constitutional crisis at this juncture. Though it may not settle the issue, it is an important step along the way.[30]

This gentle application of the WPR did not, as will be detailed in the following sections, mean that Congress had foreclosed the option of subsequently playing a strong, even confrontational, role with regard to Lebanon; it did suggest that the WPR can, if Congress and the President so desire, play a direct and positive role in the foreign policymaking process.

Withdrawal of U.S. Forces

The political coalition that had produced the MFLR began to disintegrate after the October 23 attack on the marine compound, as public support for the marines' presence in Lebanon dissolved. On Capitol Hill, the House Democratic leadership, in particular, gradually abandoned the September compromise and eventually joined those calling for the withdrawal of U.S. forces.

This congressional change of heart was also attributable to the marked deterioration in Lebanon's political situation as a whole, and to growing doubts on the part of congressional leaders that a diplomatic solution to Lebanon's problems could be found. While Republican Senators refrained from challenging the President openly, moderate Democrats in the House, who had originally supported the MFLR, voiced opinions similar to those expressed by Senate Democrats who had opposed the resolution—namely, that in the absence of a realistic diplomatic objective on the part of the Administration, the continued presence of U.S. forces in Lebanon served no useful purpose. In a letter to the President dated

December 14, 1983, Congressmen Hamilton, chairman of the Foreign Affairs Subcommittee on Europe and the Middle East, and Les Aspin (D-WI), whose support had aided passage of the MFLR, asserted that the Administration had overstated the U.S. stake in Lebanon while not doing enough to seek a negotiated solution to that country's problems. On the topic of the MNF, they sounded a clear warning: "We must resist the temptation to resort to military solutions in Lebanon . . . we should have no illusion that military options will resolve the political problems we confront in Lebanon."[31]

These men believed that the presence of the MNF in Beirut had no inherent value; it was constructive only to the extent that it facilitated political solutions. Speaker O'Neill himself left no doubt as to the practical consequences of this conclusion, declaring on January 3, 1984, that unless rapid progress were made toward a diplomatic solution, "I will join with many others in Congress in reconsidering Congressional authorization of the Marine presence in Lebanon."[32]

No diplomatic breakthrough was in the offing. Instead, conditions in Beirut continued to deteriorate, while U.S. military activities escalated to include air strikes by carrier-based aircraft. By late January, a majority of House Democrats, led by the Speaker, had resolved to take action. On February 1 the Democratic Caucus submitted a draft resolution directly to the House Foreign Affairs Committee—a highly unusual procedure— calling for the "prompt and orderly withdrawal" of the marines from Lebanon. Although this resolution was not binding, it carried considerable political weight.

Although it later became clear that the Administration was already planning to pull the marines out of Lebanon, its reaction to the draft resolution was extremely critical. In his testimony before the Foreign Affairs Committee, Assistant Secretary of State Lawrence Eagleberger predicted dire consequences should the United States retreat from the threat of terrorism, thus abandoning Lebanon to Syria and its Soviet patrons.[33] This attack apparently had the desired effect, at least momentarily. The House leadership delayed the resolution on its way to final floor consideration. Before it was released for debate, the President announced his decision to "redeploy" the marines to ships offshore, thus defusing the crisis.

In contrast to the negotiations that led to the LEAA and the MFLR, the draft resolution was an overtly partisan exercise. By passing the Speaker's proposal, House Democrats, and by implication the entire Democratic Party, would have publicly dissociated themselves from the President's increasingly unpopular Lebanon policy, setting the stage for an all-out political confrontation whose forum would have been not the Congress but rather the impending presidential election.

Even so, the institutional dimension should not be dismissed. Had U.S. involvement in Lebanon not been terminated, it is not inconceivable that congressional Republicans, especially those Senate leaders who had long been discretely critical of the President's Lebanon policy, might have concluded that their best option for self-preservation was to work out a new agreement with House Democrats—this time excluding the President. They might have gone so far as to invoke Section 7(a) of the MFLR by introducing a joint resolution calling for the withdrawal of U.S. troops. It is impossible to know what the outcome of the resulting political/institutional confrontation might have been, but it is easy to see why the President chose to avoid it.

The "Indirect" Role of Congress

Superficially, the three phases of congressional involvement in the Lebanese episode can be interpreted as illustrating different, and increasingly confrontational, types of congressional behavior. Initially, congressional leaders followed patterns that had been established in earlier presidential initiatives, invoking the ideal of war powers but taking little effective action. Among the reasons for this inaction were most Members' agreement with the President's stated goals, if not necessarily his methods, and the low profile maintained by U.S. forces throughout the first year of their presence in Beirut. By June 1983, the President's actions, as well as the Administration's objectives, were ratified retroactively with the passage of the LEAA. After August, however, congressional opposition to the President's methods increased—most importantly among Republican Senators—and the potential for confrontation arose. The MFLR compromise staved off immediate confrontation, but further deterioration in the Lebanese situation led to the open political clashes that preceded the final withdrawal of U.S. forces. At no time, however, did Congress unambiguously impose its will on the President, through the WPR or any other means.

On a deeper level, the most significant question may be the extent to which Congress limited the President's options, either overtly or implicitly. A historical perspective is important here. The Lebanon episode represented a major use of U.S. military force by post-Vietnam standards. When compared to presidential actions in the years before 1973, however, the striking feature of President Reagan's behavior is its restraint.

In analyzing the Reagan Administration's actions in Grenada, Libya, and Central America, we have noted repeatedly that the Administration showed an implicit understanding of the boundaries of acceptable military initiatives and that the provisions of the WPR, interpreted broadly, approximated this tacit agreement. The Administration's behavior in Lebanon strongly supports this conclusion and provides reason to believe that the role of Congress in maintaining the status quo established during the 1970s may have been greater than is generally recognized.

The potential for long-term escalation was arguably higher in Lebanon than in any other situation since 1973. Unlike the case in Central America, when it sent troops to Lebanon, the United States had openly deployed a combat-ready force into a hostile environment. In contrast with operations in Grenada and Libya, the U.S. objective here was not the relatively straightforward task of carrying out a discrete offensive operation, but the much more complex role of supporting an embattled government. It is possible to identify at least two distinct cases in which the option of escalating the U.S. presence was actually proposed and debated at high levels.

First, during an October 1982 visit to Washington, President Gemayel of Lebanon requested that the MNF be increased to a count of some 30,000 to be deployed throughout Lebanon.[34] The United States, in all probability, would have been called on to provide the bulk of this force. At the time, optimism still ran high concerning the prospects for a U.S.-sponsored diplomatic solution that would lead to the withdrawal of Syrian and Israeli forces from Lebanon; such a deployment might arguably have been defended as consistent with U.S. objectives in that it would assist the "legitimate" Lebanese government to maintain order as foreign troops were removed. The risks of less favorable developments go without saying. Still, it is possible to see how the deployment might have been extremely attractive to an American President. For President Reagan, however, it was never a realistic option. Key congressional leaders' grudging acceptance of the limited U.S. role in the MNF left no doubt that even Republicans such as Howard Baker, upon whom the President relied heavily for his effective control of Congress, would have openly opposed such a plan.

A second documented opportunity to expand the U.S. presence in Lebanon came in the summer of 1983, when the Israeli armed forces prepared to withdraw from positions in the Chouf Mountains overlooking the U.S. Marine positions in Beirut. In May the commander of the marines in Lebanon reportedly recommended that U.S. forces expand their area of occupation to include key positions that would be abandoned by the Israelis. Such a move, it was hoped, would prevent factional fighting that might endanger U.S. forces in these areas.[35] Once again, such a move might have been tactically sound, but by August, when the Israelis actually withdrew, the political climate in the United States clearly would not have tolerated it. Moreover, the intervening passage of the LEAA would have given congressional opponents of this latest move the means to force a public legislative showdown. With the political wind at their back, it is not inconceivable that they might have succeeded in overturning the President's decision. The Administration chose not to take the risk.

The strongest evidence for indirect but effective congressional restraint on the President's options may be found in the circumstances surrounding the ultimate withdrawal of U.S. forces from Beirut in 1984. By this time, the position of the U.S. force was untenable in purely military terms. The marines were under attack. To defend themselves effectively, they would have needed to expand the territory under their control—acquiring, in particular, the high ground overlooking the initial deployment site—and, in all likelihood, to receive substantial reinforcements. Such a move, however, even labeled "self-defense," would have been politically suicidal for the President. Widely unpopular with the electorate at large, it would almost certainly have been challenged in Congress. At the very least, the resulting political confrontation would have been out of proportion to Lebanon's potential value for U.S. foreign policy. By effectively foreclosing this possibility, Congress further narrowed the President's options, eventually leaving him with little choice but to withdraw U.S. forces.

Conclusion

In the Lebanon situation, the WPR proved valuable both as a working definition of the limits of Executive freedom of action and as a vehicle for compromise. Enactment of the MFLR marked the first time that the WPR had served as a direct means for exercising the collective judgment of the two branches as intended by the Resolution's authors. As a true compromise, the MFLR did not fully satisfy any of the parties involved in its shaping. All of them, however, came to believe that it was the best available solution at the time. It is to be hoped that this precedent will facilitate the negotiation of future comparable agreements.

The Lebanon experience also illustrated that while the WPR itself, lacking enforcement provisions, is not particularly effective for changing Executive behavior directly, the Congress has other tools available to it. The use, both actual and threatened, of purse-string restrictions in Lebanon was a reminder of the latent institutional power of the Congress and a primary motivator behind the Executive's policy of implicit compliance with the broad limits of the WPR.

The most significant conclusion, however, is a more general one. In the 1970s and 1980s, military actions undertaken by the Executive have fallen within certain definable boundaries. In Lebanon those boundaries were overtly set—and defended—by the Congress; in other cases they remained implicit but of considerable importance. Congressional actions from 1980 to 1986 suggest that while the President has nearly total flexibility within these boundaries, the Congress will challenge attempts to step beyond them.

THE REAGAN ADMINISTRATION AND THE NICARAGUAN CONTRAS

The 1984 congressional decision to cut off funding for the Nicaraguan insurgent forces known as the Contras demonstrates how effectively one House of Congress can wield its power of the purse. Moreover, it represents one of the few cases during the Reagan Administration in which institutional considerations took on an importance rivaling that of partisan and ideological alignments. More generally, the troubled history of the relationship between the United States and the Contras illustrates the extent and limits of congressional influence in covert military operations during the mid-1980s.

In its structure and institutional context, the debate over aid to the Contras presents certain parallels to the Angolan and Turkish episodes a decade earlier. In all of these cases, the focus was not on the limited issue of the WPR but on the broader question of whether Congress could enforce the ideal that a predetermined accord between the Executive and Legislative branches should be the basis of U.S. foreign policy.

Debate in 1982 and 1983: The First Boland Amendment

Contra aid was a controversial issue from the outset and, despite a major public relations effort, the President was unable to rally overwhelming public support for it at any point. As early as 1982, considerable opposition was evident among congressional Democrats, and particularly among the members of the House Intelligence Committee. In April of that year, committee members proposed in secret session to end covert aid to the Contras entirely. While the committee, at the behest of Chairman Edward Boland (D-MA), rejected the cutoff at that time, two significant restrictions were placed on the aid: U.S. funds were to be used only for the purpose of interdicting arms shipments to insurgent forces in El Salvador, and were not to be employed to overthrow the government of Nicaragua or to provoke a military exchange between Nicaragua and its neighbors.[36] This last measure, which became known as the "first Boland Amendment," was included in both the FY 1983 Intelligence Authorization Bill and the FY 1983 Continuing Resolution on Appropriations.

In fact, these restrictions did not clash with the Reagan Administration's publicly stated goals. As late as April 27, 1983, President Reagan, addressing a joint session of Congress, denied that the U.S. government sought the overthrow of the Nicaraguan government but rather was working "to prevent the flow of arms to El Salvador, Honduras, and Costa Rica."[37]

By the spring of 1983, however, Congressman Boland and the majority of the House Intelligence Committee had concluded that the Administration was not abiding by the terms of the 1982 Boland Amendment and, moreover, that the positive goal of support for the Contras—interdiction of arms shipments to El Salvador—was not being accomplished by the existing program. Consequently, Representatives Boland and Zablocki introduced a measure (H.R. 2760, 98th Cong.) to amend the Intelligence Authorization Act for FY 1983 by prohibiting further expenditures of U.S. funds "for the purpose, or which would have the effect, of supporting, directly or indirectly, military or paramilitary operations in Nicaragua by any nation, group, organization, or individual."[38] For covert aid to the Contras, the resolution substituted an overt program of aid to friendly countries in Central America to assist them in arms interdiction.

In the report that accompanied H.R. 2760, the committee elaborated on the motives and conclusions behind its actions. While indicting Cuba and Nicaragua for their extensive and effective military support of Salvadoran insurgents, the committee noted that U.S. efforts to halt the flow of arms by supporting the Contras had failed demonstrably. "The Salvadoran insurgents continue to be well armed and supplied. They have grown in number and have launched more and larger offensives. All of this requires an uninterrupted flow of arms." The committee's conclusion on this point was unequivocal. "There are certainly a number of ways to interdict arms, but deploying a sizable military force in Nicaragua is one which strains credibility."[39]

In fact, the committee concluded, providing military aid to the Contras was actually counterproductive in terms of the Administration's stated objective:

> It tends to bind the Nicaraguan population—even those with little enthusiasm for the Sandinistas—together against the threat of attack. It is the best guarantee that the free elections the executive branch says it wants will not take place, and that the Cuban influence it seeks to diminish will grow.[40]

Finally, while stopping short of accusing the Administration of illegal actions, the committee reported that it was "unwilling to assure the

House" that ongoing U.S. programs met the requirements of the 1982 Boland Amendment. It noted that the Contra groups receiving U.S. aid openly claimed to be fighting for the overthrow of the Nicaraguan government, and that their activities were clearly directed to that end—not to arms interdiction. Further, as they were not under the control of the U. S. government, there was no reason to expect that their future activities would not continue and further implement their present unacceptable plans. For all of these reasons, Boland and his colleagues concluded that a radical change of direction was called for in U.S. Central American policy, beginning with the termination of support for the Contras.

After considerable debate, the House passed H.R. 2760 by a vote of 228 to 195, with a number of conservative Democrats joining nearly all of the Republicans in opposition.[41] In the Republican-controlled Senate, however, the Intelligence Committee refused to consider the resolution. Boland and the House leadership persisted, attaching the Contra aid cutoff to the Intelligence Authorization act for FY 1984 (H.R. 2968, 98th Cong.). The Senate, however, included no analogous provision in its version of the authorization. The issue was eventually resolved in the House-Senate conference on H.R. 2968, when language was adopted limiting aid to Nicaraguan insurgents to $24 million.[42]

With this compromise, the debate over Contra aid seemed to be falling into the same pattern as that over military activities in Honduras. The Administration's policy, as usual, had the strong support of the Senate's Republican majority. A significant number of conservative Democrats in both the House and the Senate also supported it. Accordingly, while the House majority succeeded in placing certain limits and conditions on U.S. aid, the Administration largely succeeded in its basic goal of establishing and maintaining the Contras.

Boland's efforts in 1983 accomplished two major objectives nonetheless. The first was to establish a strong and coherent argument for ending aid to the Contras. This argument, as spelled out in the report to the Boland-Zablocki bill, found general acceptance in the House leadership and, in subsequent years, provided a solid position from which to attack the President's policy. The second, equally critical accomplishment was to force the issue of Contra funding into the open political arena and to establish that Congress would henceforth authorize specific dollar amounts of aid, as well as providing rules for its expenditure. Thus Boland and his allies ensured that the issue would be debated openly at least once a year, at which time Members of Congress and, in particular, the two intelligence committees, would have the opportunity to review and assess the Administration's policy.

Forcing an open accounting of the dollar amount spent on the Contras proved to be a key point, as it became apparent that support for the President's policy, even in the Senate Intelligence Committee, was not open ended. While a bipartisan majority of committee members favored the $24 million authorization for FY 1984, a number seem to have done so in the belief that the sum represented the total amount to be spent on the Contras that year—an amount generally commensurate with the limited goals claimed by the Administration and mandated by the Boland Amendment.

Accordingly, when the Administration requested an additional $21 million for the Contras in March 1984, Republican Senators began, for the first time, publicly to express doubts like those of the House Intelligence Committee. Senators William Cohen (R-ME) and David Durenberger (R-MN), both members of the Senate Intelligence Committee, while continuing to vote in favor of aid, openly warned the President that the limits on U.S. action set out in the 1983 Boland Amendment should be taken seriously. The Congress, Cohen asserted, did not support attacks against the Nicaraguan economy; the Administration must abide by legislated restrictions or risk losing congressional support. Democratic Senators were less circumspect. Senator Daniel Patrick Moynihan (D-NY) accused the Reagan Administration of seeking—in violation of the Boland Amendment—to overthrow the Nicaraguan government.[43]

Despite these uncertainties, the President and his congressional allies retained control of the issue in the Senate, as well as considerable influence in the House. This had been sufficient to ensure congressional acquiescence to Administration initiatives in El Salvador and Honduras despite opposition from House leaders. There is little reason to believe that it would not have sustained increased aid to the Contras had not an unforeseen event triggered a sharp drop in the President's credibility with his key Senate supporters.

The 1984 Mining Incident and the Cutoff of Funds

The April 1984 revelation that the CIA had been actively involved in mining Nicaraguan ports caught most Members of Congress, including the President's staunchest supporters, entirely by surprise. Despite the Administration's claims that placing the mines was an act of "collective self-defense" and was consistent with congressionally mandated guidelines relating to Nicaragua, Members of both parties expressed overwhelming disapproval. Both the House and Senate passed resolutions of condemnation—the latter by a remarkable bipartisan margin of 84 to 12.

More ominously for the Administration, many of its most influential allies reacted with outrage. Among these was the chairman of the Senate Intelligence Committee, Senator Barry Goldwater, who was angered as much by the fact that he and his committee had not been informed of the operation as by the mining itself. The Senator's indignation flared when he learned that the Democratic-controlled House Intelligence Committee had known of the CIA involvement in the mining as early as January 31. As Goldwater pointed out in a strongly worded letter to CIA Director William Casey, the Administration's tactics risked crippling the efforts of its Senate supporters.

> The President has asked us to back his foreign policy. Bill, how can we back his foreign policy when we don't know what the hell he is doing? This is an act violating international law. It is an act of war. For the life of me, I don't know how we are going to explain it.
>
> My simple guess is that the House is going to defeat the supplemental [containing the $21 million for the Contras] and we will not be in a position to put up much of an argument after we were not given the information we were entitled to receive.[44]

Senator Goldwater's legislative predictions proved to be largely accurate. The Senate approved the supplemental appropriations bill, defeating an attempt to delete Contra aid by a vote of 58 to 38. On this vote, however, key members of the Intelligence Committee voted against the Administration for the first time. Democrats Daniel Inouye (D-HI), Lloyd Bentsen (D-TX), Daniel Patrick Moynihan (D-NY), Walter Huddleston

(D-KY), and Republican William Cohen (R-ME) joined Senators Joseph Biden (D-DE) and Patrick Leahy (D-VT) in opposition.[45]

Meanwhile, the House had already voted by a margin of 241 to 177 to drop Contra aid from the supplemental appropriations bill. Once again, the House-Senate conference was the forum for a final confrontation; in the new political environment, House Members prevailed. By refusing to back down, or even to compromise, they delayed final passage of the supplemental appropriations bill until late June 1984. Finally the Senate, under considerable pressure to pass the other appropriations contained in the bill—such as a politically popular and obviously time-sensitive summer jobs program—deleted the Contra aid provision and allowed the bill to go through.[46]

Seeking to capitalize on this "tactical" advantage, Boland and the House leadership included an affirmative prohibition on any further aid to the Contras in the FY 1985 Intelligence Authorization Bill (H.R. 5399, 98th Cong.). On August 2, 1984, the House ratified this provision by a vote of 294 to 118. The final compromise with the Senate, which was written into the continuing resolution for FY 1985 (P.L. 98-473), demonstrated the ongoing weakness of the President's supporters. A total ban of aid to the Contras was applied to extend at least until February 1985, at which time the President could request $14 million. An affirmative vote of both Houses would be required to release the funds, however, giving the House an effective veto over Contra funding for all of FY 1985. This measure became known as the "second Boland Amendment."

Institutional Lessons of the 1984 Contra Debate

In considering why the House Majority succeeded in imposing its will on Contra aid in 1984, while failing to win passage of the Foley Amendment and halt military activities in Honduras during the same period, the obvious explanation is that the Administration's miscalculation in failing to inform its Senate allies of the Nicaraguan mining effectively negated the value of their support. In addition, the President's opponents had a coherent preexisting analysis of the larger issue to bolster their position, and thus were ideally placed to take advantage of the President's temporary weakness. The "tactical" lesson of the affair, then, is that in certain circumstances a single body of Congress can indeed exercise its power of the purse to block Executive policy.

There is also a more general institutional conclusion to be drawn and it applies both to the House and the Senate in this case as well as having direct relevance to the WPR. The institutional outrage that united Members of both parties against the President in the wake of the mining incident was based on the perception that the Administration, having reached a working understanding with the Congress on the goals and limits of U.S. activities in Nicaragua, had then deliberately ignored that understanding by carrying out operations of a totally different nature. This is the sentiment that moved Senator Goldwater to anger. It is very different from the policy and political considerations that had initially motivated the House leadership to oppose the President's policy—a position that, as we have seen, did not prevail on its own.

The Administration's Policy Regains Momentum

With Ronald Reagan's overwhelming reelection victory in November 1984, the political tide turned against the opponents of Contra aid, while the Administration repaired its relations with key congressional supporters. The furor over the mining incident died down and the Administration, seemingly mindful of the lessons of its recent defeats, spoke less of military measures and more of providing "humanitarian" or at least "non-lethal" assistance to the Contras. At the same time, the Administration tacitly dropped its effort to link support for the Contras to the interdiction of weapons to the insurgents in El Salvador. Instead, the Sandinista regime itself was made the focus of debate, both in terms of the security threat it posed to the United States and in the context of the Reagan Administration's broader policy of opposing Soviet-backed regimes throughout the world.

While many Members of Congress questioned the ultimate significance of the Administration's semantic shift to "non-lethal" aid, there is no doubt that the Administration's tactics as a whole, coupled with the President's newly reaffirmed political strength, threatened the position of moderate Democrats in the House who had provided the key votes in favor of the aid cutoff in 1984. While the House voted to retain the ban on Contra aid in April 1985, the leadership was unable to prevent the issue from resurfacing later that spring. On June 12 the House cast its first positive vote on Contra aid in over three years, approving $27 million in "humanitarian" assistance for FY 1985.[47]

Congressional actions in 1986 relaxed restrictions even further. After initially defeating a Contra aid bill in March 1986, the House reversed its position on June 25, after intense presidential lobbying, and approved an amendment to H.R. 5052 (the military construction authorization bill for FY 1987) providing $100 million in assistance to the Contras.[48] The Senate followed on August 13, voting along party lines to approve an identical measure. Of the funds thereby appropriated, up to $70 million could be used for military activities. Military assistance from these funds actually began reaching the Contras in October 1986.

The 1986 Contra aid bill also lifted a number of restrictions on U.S. activities that had been in force since the passage of the first Boland Amendment, most notably the ban on participation by U.S. military and intelligence personnel in assistance to the Contras. Among the few remaining restrictions were the ban on using U.S. government funds other than those specifically appropriated for the purpose—intended principally to prevent expenditures from the secret CIA contingency fund—and a measure forbidding military or civilian personnel of the U.S. government to conduct operations inside Nicaragua or to "participate directly or indirectly in the provision of any assistance to the anti-Sandinista guerrillas ... within 20 miles of the border of Nicaragua."[49]

New Reversals for the Administration

Less than a month after renewed military aid began reaching the Contras, two events in the United States threw the Reagan Administration's Nicaraguan policy into renewed jeopardy. First was the congressional election of November 1986, which returned control of the Senate to the Democratic Party for the first time in six years. This probably would have been insufficient to reverse the President's policy toward the Contras had it not been for the second event—the late-November revelation that individuals employed by the National Security Council had participated in a number of irregular activities, including providing arms to the Contras during the period when U.S. military assistance was forbidden by the 1984 Boland Amendment.

Leaving aside the question of possible illegalities those Executive branch employees may have committed, the relevance of this episode in the larger context of Legislative-Executive relations is fairly clear. As in the 1984 mining incident, the Administration knowingly took actions that went beyond congressionally mandated boundaries. And once again, these actions prompted the defection from the President's camp of moderate Members of both parties whose support for the Administration on previous occasions was attributable more to reluctance to oppose the President than to strong support for the Contras. Combined with the new balance of power in the Senate, these revelations reopened the broader debate on aid to the Contras. While the continuation of U.S. assistance for the remaining years of the Reagan Administration seemed a foregone conclusion in the autumn of 1986, it was thrown into question once again by the summer of 1987.

6 THE COLLECTIVE JUDGMENT OF CONGRESS AND THE PRESIDENT

The years from 1940 through 1970 witnessed a remarkable expansion in the war powers claimed and wielded by American Presidents. Beginning in the 1960s, Members of Congress sought with varying degrees of success first to stem and then to reverse this tide. By the late 1980s, the outline of a new balance of power between Congress and the President on the question of war powers began to emerge. The President retains the power to employ U.S. armed forces for brief operations and in noncombat situations—a power that the Executive has repeatedly exercised throughout the twentieth century—but effectively has lost the ability to commit forces to long-term conflict entirely on his own authority, as Truman did in Korea and Johnson in Vietnam. Between these two extremes, however, Justice Jackson's "zone of twilight" persists.

Moreover, the observed status quo, such as it is, exists only in practice. On the theoretical level, the controversy is as great as ever. The sweeping claims of presidential authority first made on behalf of President Truman are still maintained by his successors; the constitutional position first stated explicitly in the reports on the National Commitments Resolution of 1969 remains the position of many congressional proponents of war powers legislation.

In this context, the WPR has played a very different role than that which its authors had anticipated. Rather than serving as an accepted mechanism for legislative action, the resolution has triggered debate and provided a general definition of the outer limits of the President's freedom of action. Although falling short of original expectations, this role is far from insignificant. Even when the resolution has been invoked only partially or not at all, by its very existence it has drawn attention to presidential behavior and legislative responsibility. In this final chapter, we explore the nature of the balance of power between Congress and the President on the war powers issue as it currently exists, as well as discussing possible directions for future policy initiatives.

THE POWER TO MAKE WAR: THE STATUS QUO IN 1987

Two situations that unfolded in the autumn of 1987—U.S. naval operations in the Persian Gulf and the continuing debate over U.S. policy in Central America—illustrate the current balance of institutional power. While the President retained considerable freedom of action in the first instance, and the Congress wielded its legislative power in the second, both typify the "twilight zone" of foreign policymaking in which neither branch is willing to concede total precedence to the other.

The Power of the Commander-in-Chief

The events preceding the deployment of a vastly expanded U.S. naval force in the Persian Gulf followed a pattern similar to that observed in the early stages of America's involvement in Lebanon. U.S. policy was prompted by the request of a friendly Arab government that felt threatened by forces beyond its control—in this case the ongoing war between Iran and Iraq. The President then intitiated American military action despite reservations expressed by congressional leaders of both parties.

In January of 1987, the government of Kuwait, feeling increasingly threatened by Iranian attacks on neutral-country shipping in the Persian Gulf, approached the U.S. Government with the request that a number of Kuwaiti oil tankers be re-registered under the U.S. flag, thus entitling them to the protection of the U.S. Navy. Kuwait made similar overtures to the Soviet Union. Such a re-registration, the Kuwaitis believed, would deter further Iranian attacks against these ships, thereby safeguarding a substantial portion of Kuwait's vital oil exports.

The initial U.S. responses to Kuwait's proposal were cautious. The prospect that failing to act might lead to an increase in Soviet influence in the Gulf unchallenged by the United States, however, seems to have motivated the Administration to accept the proposal. By early March 1987, the Reagan Administration had agreed, at least in principle, to re-register eleven Kuwait tankers under the American flag and to provide U.S. naval escorts for their transits of the Persian Gulf. Congressional leaders and committees received private briefings during this time, but the policy did not spark much Legislative interest.

On May 17, however, the frigate *U.S.S. Stark*, on patrol in the Gulf, was struck by missiles fired by an Iraqi warplane, killing thirty-seven American crewmen.[1] Although the attack was eventually determined to have been accidental, this unexpected event focused the nation's attention on the U.S. naval presence in the Gulf, and particularly on the proposal to re-flag Kuwaiti tankers.

Following the *Stark* incident, the Administration insisted that the planned expansion of the U.S. role in the Gulf would proceed, with escort of re-flagged tankers to begin within a few weeks.[2] At the same time, Administration officials were eager to gain the support of congressional leaders for this policy, and to that end, held both open and private briefings for various Members and committees as well as extensive private discussions with key Members.

Although the Administration's efforts to inform the Congress were generally well received, many Members were not convinced of the wisdom of the Administration's proposed actions. At the very least, many became convinced that, as in the Lebanese case, the Administration was taking military action before having developed a coherent long-term Gulf policy. Thus, Members of both Houses sought to delay re-flagging pending the receipt of more detailed information on the Administration's overall goals and strategies.

On May 21, 1987, the Senate approved by a vote of 91 to 5 an amendment to a FY 1987 continuing appropriations bill (H.R. 1827, 100th Cong.) requiring that the Secretary of Defense submit a report to Congress concerning security in the Persian Gulf before implementing any agreement to protect re-flagged Kuwaiti tankers.[3] As indicated by the final vote, this measure attracted broad bipartisan support in the Senate. Speaking in favor of the amendment, Minority Leader Robert Dole (R-KS) stressed the necessity of formulating clear and realistic policy objectives before proceeding with formal commitments or military action, asserting that "we should make no more commitments like the Kuwaiti tanker arrangement, until we are absolutely sure that it is in our long-term interest and that the commitment can be fulfilled."[4] The clear implication of Senator Dole's position was that the Administration's actions to date, taken in advance of such a careful assessment, had been unduly precipitate. Administration reactions to this Legislative activity were mixed. On May 28, the Administration seemed to bow to congressional doubts with an announcement that re-flagging operations would be postponed indefinitely and that the Congress would receive a full report specifying the mission of U.S. forces and the rules of engagement under which they would operate.[5] At the same time, however, the President and other Administration spokesmen emphasized that the United States was committed to ensuring that freedom of navigation in the Gulf was not threatened by either Iran or the Soviet Union.[6]

This ambiguous Executive response failed to satisfy some congressional critics of the Administration's policy. On July 8 House Members went beyond simply requesting reports and took direct action to limit the President's options in the Gulf. Although an attempt to prohibit the proposed re-flagging outright failed, the House passed by a vote of 222 to 184 an amendment proposed by Congressman Mike Lowry (D-WA) to the Coast Guard authorization bill (H.R. 2324, 100th Cong.) mandating that re-flagging be delayed by ninety days.[7] Speaking in favor of the amendment, Foreign Affairs Committee Chairman Dante Fascell made explicit the assertions that had been implicit in the earlier Senate debate. The Administration, he charged, had no clear Persian Gulf policy; the proposed re-flagging of eleven Kuwaiti tankers was "ad hoc, poorly defined, and dangerous."[8] Delaying the re-flagging, Fascell hoped, would give the Administration and the Congress time to develop a more coherent policy for defending U.S. interests in the Gulf.

Just what such a policy might entail, however, was not clear. House Minority Leader Robert Michel accused the Lowry Amendment's supporters of opposing the President while proposing no constructive alternative.[9] Congressman Michel's objections did not carry the day with his House colleagues, but his point was telling. This became apparent when a group of conservative Senators mounted a filibuster against all attempts to place binding restrictions on the President's actions. While this group did not constitute a majority of the Senate, the perceived lack of an alternative to the Administration's plan seems to have made other Senators, particularly Republicans, reluctant to take the decisive action required to pass binding legislation along the lines of the Lowry Amendment.

On July 15 the Senate leadership attempted to force an end to debate on a measure, presented as an amendment to an omnibus trade bill (S. 1420, 100th Cong.), that would have delayed re-flagging for ninety days. Although a majority of Senators voted to end the procedural delay, the resulting 54 to 44 vote fell short of the 60 votes needed to invoke cloture, and the amendment was never voted on.[10] By this action, the majority of the Senate's Republicans, along with a smaller number of conservative Democrats, defined the limit of the actions they were willing to consider. While Senator Dole had publicly expressed doubts about the President's proposed policy, he and his colleagues were unwilling to oppose the Administration directly on a question involving the President's authority as commander-in-chief.

Since the Congress as a whole had failed to take binding action, the Administration was free to proceed with its plans. The escort of re-flagged tankers began on July 21, 1987. The missions did not proceed entirely without incident, however. On July 24, in the course of the first convoy, a tanker struck a floating mine, presumably planted by Iran, which caused considerable damage. More incidents followed in succeeding months. On September 21 U.S. helicopters attacked and captured an Iranian ship found to be laying mines. On October 8 U.S. helicopters returned fire from Iranian patrol boats, sinking at least one of the boats.

On October 18 a re-flagged tanker was struck by an Iranian anti-ship missile. Although the attack took place in Kuwaiti territorial waters, and the ship was thus not technically under the protection of the U.S. fleet at the time, American naval ships retaliated the following day by shelling Iranian offshore oil drilling platforms that Iran had been using as observation posts.[11]

This series of incidents convinced many Members of Congress, including some who supported the re-flagging policy, that U.S. naval forces were involved in "hostilities" and that the relevant sections of the WPR should, accordingly, be invoked. While President Reagan did submit a report following the October 18 incident, it followed the long-established pattern of citing the WPR only indirectly and carefully avoided any implication that the Executive branch believed hostilities to be underway or the oversight provisions of the WPR to be in effect.[12]

An attempt to invoke the WPR had been made following the *Stark* incident, with the introduction of H.J.Res. 296, which sought to declare "imminent hostilities" to be underway and start the sixty-day clock provision of Section 5; the measure, however, was never brought to a vote in the House. After the September and October clashes, a more concerted effort was undertaken to invoke the WPR.

This effort was concentrated in the Senate, where it was led by a group of moderate and liberal Senators including Republicans Lowell Weicker (R-CT) and Mark Hatfield (R-OR). Their attempts to pass legislation declaring explicitly that hostilities were underway and invoking the sixty-day cutoff provisions of the WPR were not successful, due largely to the continued use of delaying tactics by the Senate's more conservative Republicans. Once again, the debate on invoking the WPR showed the Senate to be deeply divided not only over the policy issue in question but also over the wisdom of the WPR itself and its applicability to this type of "borderline" situation.

In the end, the Senate passed the compromise measure, sponsored by Majority Leader Byrd and Senator John Warner (R-VA), which made no mention of the WPR (S.J.Res 194, 100th Cong.). Instead, the Byrd-Warner measure required the President to submit yet another report thirty days after the resolution's enactment, and committed the Congress to taking some unspecified action within thirty days of receiving the President's report. This later action could, in theory, consist of anything from a simple acknowledgment of the President's report to a resolution requiring that U.S. operations cease—presumably by way of a funding cutoff.

In passing the Byrd-Warner resolution, the Senate leadership sought to keep its options open for future action regarding U.S. policy in the Gulf. Given the divisions evident in that body, this may have been the most that proponents of war powers could have expected. Nevertheless, a number of observers were quick once again to conclude that passage of the Byrd-Warner resolution marked the demise of the WPR as a useful piece of legislation. While this assessment may be excessive, there can be little doubt that the Gulf debate highlighted the inherent strength of the President's position and the practical limits of congressional action in circumstances such as these.

The President and high officials of his administration speak for the nation abroad; they can, if they so choose, conduct negotiations and conclude preliminary agreements without reference to the Legislative branch. Moreover, as commander-in-chief the President holds the unquestioned practical power to order military deployments and operations. Thus the President and the Executive branch can present Congress and the nation with the fait accompli of an operation underway.

Perhaps even more important than these practical considerations are the intangible factors working to the President's advantage. Experience suggests that presidential military initiatives will be initially well received by the American public, or at least given the benefit of a doubt. Expressing strong opposition to such initiatives in their early stages, thus, is likely to be politically unrewarding for Members of Congress. Nor are Members exempt from the general tendency to "rally 'round the flag" once the flag has been committed. Only in the longer term, when the costs and consequences of a given policy become apparent, can effective congressional opposition be expected to develop.

In this context, it is easy to see why the failure to establish once and for all the legitimacy of the WPR remains problematic. So long as efforts to invoke the resolution's provisions at the outset of a military initiative are interpreted—rightly or wrongly—as attacks on the presidential initiative in question, they are likely to encounter strong opposition within the Congress itself and to gather little political support with the electorate as a whole.

The debate on the Persian Gulf demonstrated once again that it is unrealistic to expect the Congress to oppose a presidential foreign policy initiative at the outset, even if some congressional leaders, and perhaps even a majority of Members, have reservations about the wisdom of that policy. As in previous situations, the matter never escalated into a full-blown institutional confrontation between Congress and the President; limits on congressional action were largely self-imposed.

It is significant that the President was able to re-flag the Kuwaiti tankers despite the fact that his Administration was generally perceived to have been weakened politically by the results of the 1986 elections and the President's lame duck status, as well as by the Iran-Contra affair. In this particular situation, none of these problems seemed to matter a great deal; the Democratic-controlled Senate in 1987 proved to be every bit as hesitant as the Republican-controlled Senate in 1982 to confront the President as commander-in-chief.

The President is not all-powerful, however. In a slightly different circumstance, during the same period of time, the Congress and its leadership were quite willing to take advantage of the Administration's declining political fortunes to mount a direct challenge to presidential policy. The remarkable contrast between Congress' hesitance regarding the Persian Gulf situation and its assertiveness in establishing U.S. Central American policy strikingly illustrates the institutional balance of power of the late 1980s.

Congress Seizes the Initiative

The revelations of the Iran-Contra affair brought the Administration's policy toward Nicaragua to a standstill. Ironically, these revelations undermined support for the Contras in Congress just when the President had, by his efforts of public persuasion, largely overcome the problems caused by the Administration's previous blunder—the 1984 mining incident. In the wake of these events, the initiative on the Contra issue passed once again from the President to the Congress.

The extent of this shift was illustrated by the growing influence of House Speaker James Wright (D-TX). In the summer of 1987, Speaker Wright joined with President Reagan and congressional Republicans to propose a "bi-partisan peace plan" for Central America that, at least in theory, envisaged an eventual halt of U.S. military aid to the Contras.[13] The true goals and motives of the Executive branch in launching this proposal were not entirely clear at the time, and a number of observers speculated that by establishing requirements that the Nicaraguan government was not prepared to meet, the Reagan Administration was in fact maneuvering to strengthen its position in the anticipated debate on continuing Contra aid. Even if this were the case, however, the perceived need to involve the Speaker publicly illustrated the Administration's new appreciation of the difficulty of the task before it.

The question of the Reagan-Wright Plan's sincerity soon became moot when the Presidents of the five Central American nations, including Nicaragua, signed an agreement proposed by Costa Rican President Oscar Arias on August 7, 1987. This agreement, which came to be known as the Guatemala Accord, committed each of its signers to pursue a policy of democratization and national reconciliation. In practical terms this meant that the governments of Nicaragua, El Salvador, and Guatemala were to (1) initiate negotiations aimed at reaching a political settlement to insurgencies in their countries and (2) work to integrate the various opposition forces into an open and peaceful political process. Other key provisions of the accord committed the signers to cease all support of insurgent activities directed against their neighbors. If carried out in full, the agreement would lead to the expulsion of the Contras from their bases in Honduras, as well as an end to Nicaraguan support of the Salvadoran insurgents.[14]

President Reagan and other high Administration officials offered only qualified support for the Guatemala Accord and expressed their intention to request additional military aid for the Contras.[15] Speaker Wright, on the other hand, was quick to endorse the negotiating process launched by the accord.[16] Moreover, he took an active role in the ensuing diplomatic initiatives.

In November 1987 Wright met privately with leaders of both the Sandinista government and the Contras, as well as with Nicaraguan Cardinal Miguel Obando y Bravo, who had been asked by the Sandinistas to mediate between the various Nicaraguan factions. At a November 13 press conference, the Speaker announced that all of the parties involved agreed to begin negotiations to resolve the Nicaraguan insurgency.[17] Wright's success in convincing the Nicaraguan parties to negotiate with each other—a possibility that the Sandinistas had long ruled out—implied that Nicaragua accepted the fact that further U.S. aid to the Contras would hinge in large part on decisions made on Capitol Hill.

The Speaker's activities evoked angry statements but little effective action from the White House, which accused Wright of infringing on the Executive branch's prerogative to carry out diplomacy. There was, in fact, little that the Administration could do. Indeed, the Administration itself had, for all practical purposes, conceded that it was unable to force the issue. On November 10, two days before Speaker Wright's press conference, Secretary of State George Shultz had stated publicly that the Administration would not seek renewed military aid for the Contras in 1987.[18]

Had it occurred earlier in his term, President Reagan likely would have been able to block Speaker Wright's initiative and force an open confrontation on renewed Contra aid by appealing directly to Congress and the American public. Moreover, it is not inconceivable that the President would have succeeded in having aid approved, as he had in earlier confrontations with the House leadership on this issue. In 1987, however, the political balance of power had shifted. Now the Speaker, confident of the support of the rest of the House leadership, could wield effectively the institutional power that the situation afforded him.

This inherent institutional power was the key to the situation. Underlying the Speaker's newfound diplomatic prominence was an unalterable fact: the provision of further U.S. military aid to the Contras depended not only on the President but on positive congressional action. Regardless of the Administration's public pronouncements, renewed Contra aid would not be made available until and unless both Houses of Congress were convinced that the diplomatic process underway had failed. Lacking such determination, either House could block proposed aid merely by failing to act.

The Administration's Persian Gulf policy, on the other hand, could be carried out at the President's discretion until and unless the Congress took affirmative action to cut off funding for it. Congressional inaction in this case, whatever its cause, worked to the President's advantage. This critical distinction does much to explain the positions taken by the two branches and the relative success of their initiatives in each situation.

Conclusions

With these recent examples in mind, as well as the events described in previous chapters of this book, we can characterize the circumstances under which the Congress can be expected to play an effective role in influencing policy relating to the direct or indirect use of U.S. military power.

In situations involving the direct use of U.S. armed forces, the Executive branch retains nearly total freedom of action in the early stages of an operation. The power, as well as the prestige, of the President's position as commander-in-chief constitutes an institutional position that the Congress cannot match in the short term. If the President's objectives can be accomplished quickly, as was the case in the Grenada and Libya operations, this freedom of action is effectively complete. In the case of covert operations, the power and prestige of the commander-in-chief are less relevant; nonetheless, the Executive's practical ability to conduct operations secretly affords it considerable flexibility in this case as well.

When U.S. involvement, whether open or covert, continues over a period of months or years, the likelihood of congressional action can increase if public opposition to military actions develops or if covert operations become public knowledge. The methods Congress might choose to employ and the level of influence it could attain depend on a number of factors.

Obviously, the likelihood of congressional intervention is related to the cost of the operation in question as perceived by Members of Congress: witness the direct link between congressional activism and the increase in American casualties in Lebanon during 1983 and 1984. This observation could, of course, have been made with regard to almost any military operation. Casualties are never popular. What is remarkable in the 1980s is the degree to which the threshold of intervention has lowered. The level of concern and involvement that the Congress reached only after tens of thousands of American casualties in Vietnam was apparent after a tiny fraction of that number in Beirut.

Human casualties are not the only cost to which the Congress is sensitive. In Nicaragua the primary cost was political; the 1984 mining incident and the 1987 Iran-Contra affair damaged the political position of the Administration's congressional supporters, while strengthening the hand of its opponents. As a result the opponents gained sufficient influence within the Congress to wield the inherent institutional power of the Legislative branch (in this case, the ability to control funding) with considerable effect.

Consideration of human and political costs alone does not fully explain congressional behavior, however. After all, the American people and their political leaders have accepted huge sacrifices in past wars. Whether such sacrifices will be tolerated in any given case depends largely on the relative strength and coherence of the overall strategic vision underlying the Administration's policy. If the Administration's motives and goals are generally understood and command widespread public support, its methods are much less likely to be questioned.

A recent illustration of this point is provided by the overwhelmingly positive reaction to the Administration's policy toward Libya. The naval buildup which preceded the 1986 air strike against Tripoli was never seriously challenged, even when it led to clashes between U.S. and Libyan naval and air units. The President's assertion that such actions were a necessary and appropriate response to Libyan-backed terrorism was generally accepted; support for the military action followed. It is not unreasonable to speculate that this support would have continued even if the operations had resulted in significant American casualties.

This unity of purpose contrasts with the lengthy and often acrimonious debate that surrounded Administration initiatives in Lebanon and Central America. Here the Administration's publicly expressed goals and strategic vision proved less convincing, leaving its policy vulnerable to congressional opposition, which crystallized when the cost became too high.

A final consideration is the success of the Administration's opponents in formulating and expressing an alternative policy, or at minimum a persuasive critique of the President's policy. In the cases cited above, congressional leaders' ability to influence the Administration's policy in Lebanon and Nicaragua was largely attributable to the existence of an established critique of that policy on which to base their own actions. The lack of such an alternative position for the Administration's initiatives in Honduras and El Salvador—along with the lower perceived cost of these actions—does much to explain the relative lack of success enjoyed by congressional opponents of these policies. A similar pattern seemed to be developing with regard to U.S. initiatives in the Persian Gulf in 1987. In contrast, the emergence of the Guatemala Accord on Central America in the summer of 1987 gave congressional leaders the opportunity to do more than merely oppose Administration initiatives by providing a competing policy alternative they could support.

If and when a working majority of the Congress is prepared to act, there remains the problem of means. Congressional power is greatest when the Administration must request specific appropriation of funds in order to carry out a particular activity. In such a case, opposition by a majority of even a single House of Congress is sufficient, at least in theory, to reverse presidential policy, since failure to take any legislative action at all will leave the desired activity unfunded.[19] Moreover, it is possible in such instances for a congressional majority not only to decide whether a given activity should be carried out but also to mandate binding guidelines and restrictions for it. The various restrictions on U.S. activities in Nicaragua prior to the 1984 funding cutoff exemplify such a legislative action as, to a lesser extent, did the Lebanon Emergency Assistance Act of 1983.

A more difficult situation arises when Members of Congress seek to prohibit the use of previously appropriated funds for a given purpose. Since affirmative legislation is required for this, both Houses must act in concert. Moreover, as the experience of the early 1970s demonstrated, the size of the U.S. military budget and the President's ability to shift spending from one purpose to another make such actions difficult at best. They are, nevertheless, possible, and as such remain Congress' ultimate weapon when dealing with a recalcitrant Executive. Even the implied threat of a funding cutoff, for example, enabled the Congress to serve as an effective focal point for the rising general opposition to the presence of U.S. forces in Beirut in late 1983 and early 1984, although no direct congressional action was taken to force withdrawal.

A major limitation of actions of this sort, for all their potential power, is that they are directly useful only as instruments of all-out opposition to presidential policy. When congressional majorities seek only to influence or limit Administration initiatives already under way, rather than reversing them entirely, the institutional position of the Legislative branch is much weaker. This is the very problem that the WPR was intended to address. For all of the reasons explored in this book, however, the problem persists even today.

Thus, although the present balance of Executive-Legislative power shows a remarkable change from the nearly total Executive dominance of foreign policy between World War II and Vietnam, few observers would conclude that it represents an ideal situation. The level of interbranch tension remains high, and the potential for institutional deadlock persists. To a certain extent, this is the natural product of the American system of separation of powers. Yet it is also largely the legacy of more recent events. In this context, it seems reasonable to seek solutions through a reevaluation of the WPR—the most direct legislative product of the Vietnam War and the most systematic attempt to codify the lessons of that experience.

DIRECTIONS FOR THE FUTURE

The authors of the WPR hoped that their resolution would provide a working procedure for Congress and the President to adopt whenever U.S. armed forces were deployed abroad. Clearly, this has not happened. Since the resolution's passage in 1973, interaction between the Executive and Legislative branches regarding most deployments has been confrontational rather than cooperative. The theoretical debate between Congress and the President on the issue of war powers remains open, leaving the resolution of any given political confrontation on this issue to be determined by the balance of power existing at the time and the circumstances of the particular situation. The consequences for U.S. foreign policy have not been positive.

As matters now stand, it is entirely possible for the President to commit at least a limited number of U.S. armed forces to actual or imminent hostilities on his own authority as commander-in-chief and, having made that initial commitment, to expand it within fairly broad limits. The President lacks, however, the power to sustain such an initiative indefinitely. As time passes and costs mount, the Congress may well become willing and able to force a policy reversal, as experience has proven more than once.

Allowed to operate unabated, this dynamic can be expected to lead to overly precipitous initiatives—as Presidents seek to establish a commitment before Congress can act—followed, after a period of months or years, by a forced retreat carried through with little regard for the initiative's initial objectives. This is the pattern of the Vietnam War. In miniature, it is the pattern of the 1982–84 U.S. intervention in Lebanon. There is no assurance that it will not play itself out once again in the U.S. involvement in the Persian Gulf.

In seeking to improve this situation, one fact is clear: we cannot go backward. A return to the days of Executive supremacy is not a realistic option. The bipartisan foreign policy consensus of the Truman and Eisenhower years, to the extent that it ever existed, was a casualty of the Vietnam War. The post-Vietnam record demonstrates convincingly that if they are left out of the policymaking process, Members of Congress can and will challenge presidential military commitments with whatever means are at hand, and that some Members at least will benefit politically from having done so.

Moreover, the international strategic environment has changed. The attack on the *U.S.S. Stark* is only a recent reminder of the new reality. Using U.S. armed forces as a political instrument has grown riskier. The days when U.S. forces could be deployed to the Dominican Republic or to Lebanon without coming under attack are gone. In these changed circumstances, the American people and their representatives in Congress will no doubt continue to demand a significant role in any decision that might lead to the use of military force abroad.

The task at hand for America's leaders is to develop a framework that allows each branch of government to contribute positively and constructively to the foreign policymaking process. Our exploration of the present situation and its shortcomings suggests a number of options to consider. If the WPR is to become more directly effective, several related but distinct problems must be solved. A path must be found around the theoretical impasse presented by the conflicting interpretations of the constitutional role of the President as commander-in-chief. In addition, claims of congressional authority must be brought into line with the realities of congressional power. Finally and most importantly, structures and precedents must be established to facilitate interbranch cooperation whenever possible.

The Role of the President

We had occasion above to note that the nearly total control of foreign policy exercised by Presidents from Truman through Nixon is no longer a realistic option. We should not be unaware, however, that a genuine and permanent increase in effective presidential power has taken place in the twentieth century. Any policy mechanism seeking long-term stability must accept this fact, implicitly if not explicitly. In practice, this means yielding to the President an unchallenged power—namely, the right to make the initial decision to deploy U.S. armed forces, whether into hostilities or otherwise, according to his sole judgment of the situation.

This course of action suggests itself for both practical and theoretical reasons. Most obviously, experience suggests that there is little that the Congress can do to check presidential uses of military power in the very early stages of any operation; the institutional and political advantages lie entirely with the Executive. To seek to legislate otherwise is, at best, of doubtful value.

More important, it is not at all clear that strict prior restrictions on presidential action, if they could actually be enacted and enforced, would be in the nation's best interest. A strong case can be made for the proposition that the only coherent foreign policy that can successfully be legislated in advance is isolationism; the record of U.S. history would seem to support this argument. It is not a coincidence that periods of congressional dominance in American government have tended to be synchronized with an isolationist foreign policy; the 1870s–80s and the 1930s stand as examples.[20] If the United States is to act effectively as a leader in world affairs, its government must retain enough flexibility to be able to act quickly and decisively. To take such action is properly the role of the Executive.

In terms of the WPR, this conclusion entails fully accepting Zablocki's position as opposed to Eagleton's on the question of prior restraints, and abandoning Section 2(c)—the truncated enumeration of presidential powers—which contains the echo of Eagleton's position. Such a move, which would not diminish the resolution's operative provisions, would have the dual benefit of removing a source of ambiguity and misunderstanding and of depriving the Executive of an obvious target for attack.

Congressional Oversight; Proposals for the Long Term

If history suggests the limitations of congressional government, the more recent past leaves little doubt as to the dangers of unchecked Executive adventurism. While conceding to the President the primary responsibility for initiating military action, thus, it is critical to consider how most effectively to ensure congressional participation at the earliest possible stage of any initiative.

The authors of the WPR sought to achieve this through the automatic sixty- to ninety-day deadline in Section 5(b). Of all of the resolution's provisions, however, this one has made the least progress toward acceptance, let alone effective implementation. Moreover, it has proven to be a major obstacle blocking general acceptance of the WPR as a whole.

This is largely attributable to a rather dubious reinterpretation of the resolution's intent. Again and again, the requirement that Congress approve any action within sixty days has been transformed into the threat that, were the WPR to be invoked, U.S. operations would automatically end in sixty days' time, and this threat then used as a pretext to avoid invoking the WPR at all.

If this claim were made only by the Executive branch, the result would long since have been an institutional confrontation and a decisive test of strength. A substantial number of legislators have also held this view, however, transforming any debate on invocation of the WPR into one on the merits of the operation in question. For the reasons explored in the preceding section, such debates are most often won by the President and his supporters. Thus, options for congressional invocation and enforcement of Section 5(b), have remained generally unexplored.

At the same time, another aspect of this question also merits concern. We have noted that, in the time immediately following a U.S. military operation, congressional sentiment tends to be highly supportive of the President.[21] Given that, it is not unreasonable to speculate that if a vote were forced under Section 5(b), the result, far from a call for withdrawal, might very well be a sweeping—and binding—endorsement of the President's action, which the Congress might well later regret.

Both of these considerations—the fact that the sixty-day cutoff has proven entirely unacceptable to the Executive branch and the possibility that it might be used to rush the Congress into a premature endorsement of military action—argue in favor of the reconsideration of the automatic cutoff. To wait and observe, while keeping open as many options as possible, is not always unproductive for the Congress, so long as it is clear that the Legislative branch is fully informed and has the power to act if and when it chooses.

Recent history leaves little doubt as to where the actual power of the Congress lies in these matters; if the Congress is to defend its claims of constitutional responsibility, its most effective instrument is the power of the purse. What remains is to develop practical means by which this power can be constructively wielded while avoiding the pitfalls we have noted. Ideally, Congress' power of the purse should be linked more explicitly to its claims of constitutional authority in questions of war and peace.

A 1977 proposal along this line, made by Senator Eagleton and Congressman Solarz, would have added to Article 5 of the WPR the provision that all funding for a given military operation would cease automatically after ninety days if the Congress had not taken statutory action in accordance with the WPR.[22] Although hearings were held, this proposal was opposed by many of the principal authors of the WPR and was never seriously considered. As noted above, the very nature of the compromise that had produced the WPR made it virtually impossible to make such a sweeping change at that time.

For those who hold that the power to initiate the use of military force belongs exclusively to the Congress, such a measure would, if successfully implemented, represent the achievement in fact of a claim heretofore made only in theory. The objections presented above to the principle of a mandatory time limit apply all the more to this proposal, however, along with the limitations inherent in post hoc funding cutoffs. In any case, there is no reason to believe that such a measure would be approved by a majority of the Congress, let alone by the Executive branch, within the foreseeable future.

It may be possible, nonetheless, to find a more constructive method of linking fiscal control to war powers. We have noted that the Congress' power is exercised most effectively when the President knows in advance that he will be required to request congressional funding for a particular activity. Not only does the Legislative branch have the option of denying funding altogether in such cases, but it can, by writing explicit limitations into appropriations, have a considerable impact on how operations are actually carried out. Moreover, the Administration, in such a case, has a powerful incentive to hold extensive consultations before initiating operations.

If the Legislative branch is to play a significant and constructive role in decisions concerning the use of military force, it would be to its advantage to institutionalize the procedure to the greatest extent possible. At present, it is entirely possible for operations such as the marine deployment in Beirut or the escort of re-flagged Kuwaiti tankers to be conducted for months or even years without specific congressional appropriation. Working to alter this state of affairs would be a logical goal for congressional proponents of legislative war powers.

Budgetary reform that defined more precisely the uses to which funds appropriated for national defense could be put would greatly strengthen the Legislative branch's institutional position. While such reform is not currently on the legislative agenda, it may not be inherently unattainable. The larger issue of budgetary reform is very much alive in the late 1980s; defense budgeting procedures were significantly changed in 1986. The time may come when more extensive changes are considered seriously.

It would be neither practical nor desirable to restrict operational funding to predefined specific activities, as is done in the case of funding for military procurement, but it should be possible to mandate that operational funds not be used for any activity requiring a report under Section 4 of the WPR. To be workable, of course, such a requirement would demand that the numerous ambiguities in the WPR's reporting requirements (detailed in Chapter 3) be resolved. Including within the law itself the explanations and examples now found only in congressional committee reports would go far to meet this goal.

Accompanying the restrictions on the use of general funds would be the creation of a contingency fund specifically ear-marked for non-routine military activities. This fund would be large enough to carry out an operation on the scale of the 1983 intervention in Grenada or to sustain operations such as the escort of re-flagged tankers for several months, and it would be available for use at the President's discretion. Employment of these monies, however, would require the President to submit within forty-eight hours of the start of any operation a report to the Congress expressly invoking the appropriate section of the WPR.

Strengthening the President's incentive to report to Congress would have value of its own. In addition to informing the Congress and the public of the Administration's goals and methods, presidential reports serve as a useful springboard for congressional debate. Moreover, these presidential reports would, under certain circumstances, trigger additional provisions.

Military initiatives for which further appropriations were required after depletion of the standing contingency fund, or any action undertaken pursuant to Section 4(a)(1) of the WPR, indicating actual or imminent hostilities, would activate more detailed oversight provisions. These would not include an automatic cutoff date; rather, they would be tied more directly to Congress' appropriation power. Such a system would compel the Administration to come before Congress and defend its policies from the outset, and to continue to do so regularly. Congress, for its part, would have a ready vehicle in the required supplementary appropriations to direct or limit the Administration's policy, if a majority of lawmakers chose to do so. Thus, Members would have both constructive options for influencing events short of all-out opposition to the President's policy and a means for expressing support for the President short of issuing a congressional blank check.

The provisions of this hypothetical oversight system are designed to correct a number of weaknesses in the WPR that have become apparent over time. In particular they would provide a means of strengthening the constructive role of the Congress while avoiding the counterproductive constitutional debate that has plagued the WPR in its present form.

Under such a regime, there would be no question of the President's power and authority as commander-in-chief to repel sudden attacks on the United States or on American armed forces abroad, or to carry out antiterrorist or hostage rescue missions. Moreover, the system would recognize the power, long wielded in practice, of the President to conduct brief military operations such as the air strike launched against Libya in 1986. Even more extensive operations, such as the 1983 U.S. intervention in Grenada, might not absolutely require prior congressional approval.

Those who hold the view, championed by Senator Thomas Eagleton, that virtually any decision relating to the use of military power must be made only by the Congress will no doubt conclude that the leeway afforded the Executive under such a system would be excessive. As we have noted, however, presidential operations of this magnitude have been undertaken throughout most of this century; to recognize them in theory is only to accept what has already been conceded in fact. More important, such recognition might enable a President to accept that system willingly, restoring the element of cooperation in policymaking that the authors of the WPR rightly considered to be crucial.

In any case, we must remember that minor military operations were not what the authors of the WPR were addressing. The example before them was the Vietnam War; it was to prevent the repetition of presidential wars of this magnitude that they worked. Reformers of the resolution would do well to keep this goal in mind. The system outlined above seeks to achieve it by providing an oversight mechanism through which congressional participation in the control of large-scale operations can be established at the earliest possible stage and maintained on a regular and coherent basis.

Using a fiscal mechanism as the means of congressional oversight would also have the enormous advantage of being enforceable, a quality sadly lacking in the WPR's present oversight provisions. The power of the Legislative branch to direct how appropriated funds shall be spent is clearly established in the Constitution and has been enforced on numerous occasions. By employing it in this case, the Congress would be following a well-known and largely successful parliamentary practice.

Perhaps the greatest benefit of the reformed oversight system would be an indirect one; under such a regime, the President would have much more incentive to engage in extensive and meaningful consultation with the Legislative branch before launching any military initiative. No President willingly courts defeat before Congress. If the Administration knows in advance that it can pursue a desired policy only if positive congressional action is forthcoming, it can be expected to explore congressional sentiments, informing and involving the Congress in the process. If, on the other hand, the Administration knows that it possesses the independent means to carry out its policy, consultation takes on a much more superficial character.

Given the current political climate, there is little reason to believe that reform of this magnitude will be considered soon. If, however, a future President sought to return to the tactics of institutional confrontation that marked the late 1960s and early 1970s, such a proposal might become relevant. More probably, the threat of action along this line could be expected to act as a powerful deterrent to renewed Executive imperialism.

Improving Consultation; Priorities for the Near Term

The system of oversight outlined above is intended to encourage communication between the Executive and Legislative branches. If adopting the system as a whole is not feasible at present, however, there remain positive steps that could be taken relatively easily. In particular, the Legislative branch could make it easier for the President to engage in timely and significant consultation, or at least give him fewer excuses for failing to do so. One of the most frequently suggested and most sensible reforms to that end is the establishment of a standing group of Members to consult regularly with the President.

Several proposals have been made since the late 1960s as to how such a group might be created and organized. In 1973 Representative Clement Zablocki introduced a bill (H.R. 8735, 93d Cong.) to create a Joint Committee on National Security. Patterned after the Joint Economic Committee, this body was to be comprised of senior Members of the House and Senate. It was to have no legislative duties, its principal function being to provide a manageable forum for regular consultation between the President and congressional leaders. Although the proposal received support from a number of key Members and, subsequently, officials of the Ford Administration, it never reached the floor of either House.[23] The intricate network of compromises and vested interests that prevented clarifying amendments to the WPR stifled Zablocki's initiative at that time.

More recently, Senator Robert Byrd introduced a resolution (S.J.Res. 340, 99th Cong.) that would have amended the WPR by designating a specific group of legislators to be consulted.[24] Once again, however, no legislative action was taken. Congress' reluctance to consider such a measure is particularly unfortunate, since this is the one significant improvement to the WPR that, in all likelihood, could be made without Executive opposition.

All Presidents have claimed willingness in principle to consult with Congress on major foreign policy questions. Consultation does not infringe on the constitutional rights or the perceived prerogatives of either branch. The objections that Presidents have voiced in particular cases have been of a practical nature—problems with security and the difficulty of gathering congressional leaders on short notice. The designation of a standing body would contribute to correcting these problems.

In order to promote efficiency and to minimize security risk, such a group should be relatively small. The eighteen Members designated in Senator Byrd's proposal probably represent an upper limit. In addition, the group should have three essential characteristics: authority, expertise, and representativeness.

To the greatest extent possible, the panel should be able to speak credibly for the Congress as a whole, giving the President an accurate idea of the likely reactions of the larger bodies, and should be able to reach and uphold at least preliminary agreements with the President. The leadership of the two Houses is the obvious example of such a group.

The panel members should also have a firm technical knowledge of the issues in question (which the established leadership may lack), so as to contribute meaningfully to debate with Executive branch experts. Members of one or more of the specialized committees of the two Houses (Foreign Affairs, Foreign Relations, Armed Services, Intelligence) should accordingly be included on the panel. The panel should also be given necessary staff and informational support.

Finally, an effective consultative body must be representative of the Congress as a whole. The experience of the early 1970s reminds us that it is all too possible for the congressional leadership to be co-opted by the Executive and lose touch with the majority of Members. The election of members to the consultative panel from the floor, or perhaps from the Democratic and Republican caucuses of the two Houses, as well as provisions for rotating panel membership, would help ensure the representativeness and thereby the authority of a consultative panel.

Creating a panel along these lines would undoubtedly advance the consultation provisions of the WPR. It would not, however, necessarily require amending the resolution itself. Freestanding legislation, or even changes in House or Senate rules, would suffice. Once established, the panel could meet regularly with the President and his advisors, rather than delaying communication until a moment of crisis is at hand. In this way, congressional leaders would be informed directly of the Administration's evolving goals and priorities while there was time to consider options and alternatives, and the President would benefit from the leaders' political advice and judgment.

Indeed, the President would reap considerable advantages from regular consultations. Politically, a President could protect himself in the event of a foreign policy failure. President Carter, to cite only one example, was particularly vulnerable to criticism following the failure of the 1980 Iranian hostage rescue mission because his Administration had refused to engage in even the most cursory consultation. Having made his decision alone, the President was assessed the full blame for its failure. Had congressional leaders been more closely involved in the decision-making before the event, they would have been less free to criticize it afterwards.

More generally, increased legislative participation in prior planning would almost certainly reduce the likelihood of counterproductive congressional "meddling" after an operation is underway. It is when the Executive branch seeks to deny Congress its legitimate role that it invites legislative trespass into foreign policy micro-management. The legislated prohibitions on U.S. reinvolvement in Southeast Asia, the Turkish Arms Embargo, and the abrupt termination of assistance to insurgents in Angola and Nicaragua all can be seen as expressions of congressional exasperation when faced with Administrations that seemed determined to deny Congress any role whatsoever.

Conclusion: The Ideal of Codetermination

American foreign policy is most effective when it is backed by a working consensus between the Executive and Legislative branches. As we have seen, however, such harmony is by no means an automatic achievement. The system of separation of powers creates tension among the branches of government; indeed, this is largely by design. Nowhere is this tension so apparent as in the area of war powers, where the Constitution's assignment of discrete areas of responsibility is, as we have seen, less than clear. But this tension need not lead to destructive confrontation. The differences between the Executive and Legislative branches can be complementary, with each correcting counterproductive tendencies of the other.

Experience has shown that the ability, let alone the will, of the Congress to create and implement a positive foreign policy is virtually nil. The record of the period of Executive supremacy, however, does not merit the conclusion that such a system is always in the best interests of the nation either. Neither Presidents nor their advisors are demonstrably less fallible than other mortals. Moreover the decision-making atmosphere of the White House, as recent events have once again demonstrated, can be conducive to self-perpetuating errors. The necessarily open and political environment of the Congress can help to correct this.

Of all of the branches of the federal government, the Congress most closely mirrors the complexities and contradictions of the electorate as a whole. Ideally, the President speaks for the majority of voters. The Congress, however, also represents the varied and often divergent groups and constituencies that comprise the American people. While this may not always promote efficiency, it is the natural and invaluable outcome of representative government.

Recent Congresses have made it clear that unchallenged Executive dominance is no longer a realistic option; legislators do not intend to stop striving for influence on foreign and security policy. The record of U.S. foreign policy since 1970 demonstrates, moreover, that Members of Congress, for better or worse, have the practical power to cripple Executive initiatives, even if they have no coherent policies to replace the Administration's rejected program.

The American system of government does not force a resolution to an interbranch crisis. The Congress cannot reject the President by a vote of no confidence, nor can he dissolve the legislative body. A serious interbranch crisis, however, paralyzes policymaking for an extended period of time, resulting in a foreign policy that is, at best, erratic and, at worst, nonexistent.

If the United States is to have an effective foreign policy, the two political branches must act in concert in times of crisis; there is no alternative. In the end, then, the most workable solution to the war powers issue focuses on the imperative and overriding need for codetermination. Both Congress and the President must play a positive role in forming and implementing foreign policy if it is to be conducted in the best interests of the American nation.

APPENDIX

TEXT OF THE WAR POWERS RESOLUTION

JOINT RESOLUTION
Concerning the war powers of Congress and the President

Resolved by the Senate and House of Representatives of the United States in Congress assembled,

SHORT TITLE

Sec. 1. This joint resolution may be cited as the "War Powers Resolution".

PURPOSE AND POLICY

Sec. 2. (a) It is the purpose of this joint resolution to fulfill the intent of the framers of the Constitution of the United States and insure that the collective judgment of both the Congress and the President will apply to the introduction of United States Armed Forces into hostilities, or into situations where imminent involvement in hostilities is clearly indicated by the circumstances, and to the continued use of such forces in hostilities or in such situations.

(b) Under article I, section 8, of the Constitution, it is specifically provided that the Congress shall have the power to make all laws necessary and proper for carrying into execution, not only its own powers but also all other powers vested by the Constitution in the Government of the United States, or in any department or officer thereof.

(c) The constitutional power of the President as Commander-in-Chief to introduce United States Armed Forces into hostilities, or into situations where imminent involvement in hostilities is clearly indicated by the circumstances, are exercised only pursuant to (1) a declaration of war, (2) specific statutory authorization, or (3) a national emergency created by attack upon the United States, its territories or possessions, or its armed forces.

CONSULTATION

Sec. 3. The President in every possible instance shall consult with Congress before introducing United States Armed Forces into hostilities or into situations where imminent involvement in hostilities is clearly indicated by the circumstances, and after every such introduction shall consult regularly with the Congress until United States Armed Forces are no longer engaged in hostilities or have been removed from such situations.

REPORTING

Sec. 4. (a) In the absence of a declaration of war, in any case in which United States Armed Forces are introduced—

(1) into hostilities, or into situations where imminent involvement in hostilities is clearly indicated by the circumstances;

(2) into the territory, airspace, or waters of a foreign nation while equipped for combat, except for deployments which relate solely to supply, replacement, repair or training of such forces; or

(3) in numbers which substantially enlarge United States Armed Forces equipped for combat already located in a foreign nation;

the President shall submit within 48 hours to the Speaker of the House of Representatives and to the President pro tempore of the Senate a report, in writing, setting forth—

(A) the circumstances necessitating the introduction of United States Armed Forces;

(B) the constitutional and legislative authority under which such introduction took place; and

(C) the estimated scope and duration of the hostilities or involvement.

(b) The President shall provide such other information as the Congress may request in the fulfillment of its constitutional responsibilities with respect to committing the Nation to war and to the use of United States Armed Forces abroad.

(c) Whenever United States Armed Forces are introduced into hostilities or into any situation described in subsection (a) of this section, the President shall, so long as such armed forces continue to be engaged in such hostilities or situation, report to the Congress periodically on the status of such hostilities or situation as well as on the scope and duration of such hostilities or situation, but in no event shall he report to the Congress less often than once every six months.

CONGRESSIONAL ACTION

Sec. 5. (a) Each report submitted pursuant to section 4(a)(1) shall be transmitted to the Speaker of the House of Representatives and to the President pro tempore of the Senate on the same calender day. Each report so transmitted shall be referred to the Committee on Foreign Affairs of the House of Representatives and to the Committee on Foreign Relations of the Senate for appropriate action. If, when the report is transmitted, the Congress has adjourned sine die or has adjourned for any period in excess of three calendar days, the Speaker of the House of Representatives and the President pro tempore of the Senate, if they deem it advisable (or if petitioned by at least 30 percent of the membership of their respective House) shall jointly request the President to convene

Congress in order that it may consider the report and take appropriate action pursuant to this section.

(b) Within sixty calendar days after a report is submitted or is required to be submitted pursuant to section 4(a)(1), whichever is earlier, the President shall terminate any use of United States Armed Forces with respect to which such a report was submitted (or required to be submitted), unless the Congress (1) has declared war or has enacted a specific authorization for such use of United States Armed Forces, (2) has extended by law such sixty-day period, or (3) is physically unable to meet as a result of an armed attack upon the United States. Such sixty-day period shall be extended for not more than an additional thirty days if the President determines and certifies to the Congress in writing that unavoidable military necessity respecting the safety of United States Armed Forces requires the continued use of such armed forces in the course of bringing about a prompt removal of such forces.

(c) Notwithstanding subsection (b), at any time that United States Armed Forces are engaged in hostilities outside the territory of the United States, its possessions and territories without a declaration of war or specific statutory authorization, such forces shall be removed by the President if the Congress so directs by concurrent resolution.

CONGRESSIONAL PRIORITY PROCEDURES FOR JOINT RESOLUTION OR BILL

Sec. 6. (a) Any joint resolution or bill introduced pursuant to section 5(b) at least thirty calendar days before the expiration of the sixty-day period specified in such section shall be referred to the Committee on Foreign Affairs of the House of Representatives or the Committee on Foreign Relations of the Senate, as the case may be, and such committee shall report one such joint resolution or bill, together with its recommendations, not later than twenty-four calendar days before the expiration of the sixty-day period specified in such section, unless such House shall otherwise determine by the yeas and nays.

(b) Any joint resolution or bill so reported shall become the pending business of the House in question (in the case of the Senate the time for debate shall be equally divided between the proponents and the opponents), and shall be voted on within three calendar days thereafter, unless such House shall otherwise determine by yeas and nays.

(c) Such a joint resolution or bill passed by one House shall be referred to the committee of the other House named in subsection (a) and shall be reported out not later than fourteen calendar days before the expiration of the sixty-day period specified in section 5(b). The joint resolution or bill so reported shall become the pending business of the House in question and shall be voted on within three calendar days after it has been reported, unless such House shall otherwise determine by yeas and nays.

(d) In case of any disagreement between the two Houses of Congress with respect to a joint resolution or bill passed by both Houses, conferees shall be promptly appointed and the committee of conference shall make and file a report with respect to such resolution or bill not later than four calendar days before the expiration of the sixty-day period specified in section 5(b). In the event the conferees are unable to agree within 48 hours, they shall report back to their respective Houses in disagreement. Notwithstanding any rule in either House concerning the printing of conference reports in the Record or concerning any delay in the consideration of such reports, such report shall be acted on by both Houses not later than the expiration of such sixty-day period.

CONGRESSIONAL PRIORITY PROCEDURES FOR CONCURRENT RESOLUTION

Sec. 7. (a) Any concurrent resolution introduced pursuant to section 5(c) shall be referred to the Committee on Foreign Affairs of the House of Representatives or the Committee on Foreign Relations of the Senate, as the case may be, and one such concurrent resolution shall be reported out by such committee together with its recommendations within fifteen calendar days, unless such House shall otherwise determine by the yeas and nays.

(b) Any concurrent resolution so reported shall become the pending business of the House in question (in the case of the Senate the time for debate shall be equally divided between the proponents and the opponents) and shall be voted on within three calendar days thereafter, unless such House shall otherwise determine by yeas and nays.

(c) Such a concurrent resolution passed by one House shall be referred to the committee of the other House named in subsection (a) and shall be reported out by such committee together with its recommendations within fifteen calendar days and shall thereupon become the pending business of such House and shall be voted on within three calendar days, unless such House shall otherwise determine by yeas and nays.

(d) In case of any disagreement between the two Houses of Congress with respect to a concurrent resolution passed by both Houses, conferees shall be promptly appointed and the committee of conference shall make and file a report with respect to such concurrent resolution within six calendar days after the legislation is referred to the committee of conference. Notwithstanding any rule in either House concerning the printing of conference reports in the Record or concerning any delay in the consideration of such reports, such report shall be acted on by both Houses not later than six calendar days after the conference report is filed. In the event the conferees are unable to agree within 48 hours, they shall report back to their respective Houses in disagreement.

INTERPRETATION OF JOINT RESOLUTION

Sec. 8. (a) Authority to introduce United States Armed Forces into hostilities or into situations where involvement in hostilities is clearly indicated by the circumstances shall not be inferred—

(1) from any provision of law (whether or not in effect before the date of the enactment of this joint resolution), including any provision contained in any appropriation Act, unless such provision specifically authorizes the introduction of United States Armed Forces into hostilities or into such situations and states that it is intended to constitute specific statutory authorization within the meaning of this joint resolution; or

(2) from any treaty heretofore or hereafter ratified unless such treaty is implemented by legislation specifically authorizing the introduction of United States Armed Forces into hostilities or into such situations and stating that it is intended to constitute specific statutory authorization within the meaning of this joint resolution.

(b) Nothing in this joint resolution shall be construed to require any further specific statutory authorization to permit members of United States Armed Forces to participate jointly with members of the armed forces of one or more foreign countries in the headquarters operations of high-level military commands which were established prior to the date of enactment of this joint resolution and pursuant to the United Nations Charter or any treaty ratified by the United States prior to such date.

(c) For purposes of this joint resolution, the term "introduction of United States Armed Forces" includes the assignment of members of such armed forces to command, coordinate, participate in the movement of, or accompany the regular or irregular military forces of any foreign country or government when such military forces are engaged, or there exists an imminent threat that such forces will become engaged in hostilities.

(d) Nothing in this joint resolution—

(1) is intended to alter the constitutional authority of the Congress or of the President, or the provisions of existing treaties; or

(2) shall be construed as granting any authority to the President with respect to the introduction of United States Armed Forces into hostilities or into situations wherein involvement in hostilities is clearly indicated by the circumstances which authority he would not have had in absence of this joint resolution.

SEPARABILITY CLAUSE

Sec. 9. If any provision of this joint resolution or the application thereof to any person or circumstance is held invalid, the remainder of the joint resolution and the application of such provision to any other person or circumstance shall not be affected thereby.

EFFECTIVE DATE

Sec. 10. This joint resolution shall take effect on the date of its enactment.

NOTES

CHAPTER 1: A ZONE OF TWILIGHT

1. U.S. Congress, Senate, *Congressional Record*, 100th Cong., October 21, 1987, p. S14655. The text of S.J. Res. 194 is printed in ibid., p. S14657. (All citations to the *Congressional Record* in this book are to the daily editions. Bound volumes of the *Record* are paginated differently.)
2. For details of the final debate on S.J. Res. 194, see ibid., pp. S14630–56.
3. See, for example, *Washington Post*, 24 September 1987, pp. A27, A33.
4. Charles Lofgren, "War-making under the Constitution, the Original Understanding," *Yale Law Journal* 81 (March 1972): 673.
5. Ibid., p. 672.
6. Cited in U.S. Congress, Senate, Committee on Foreign Relations, *War Powers*, 93d Cong., S. Rep. 220, p. 11 (hereafter cited as S. Rep. 93-220).
7. U.S. Library of Congress, Congressional Research Service, *Instances of the Use of United States Armed Forces Abroad, 1789–1983*, ed. Ellen Collier, (Washington, D.C.: Congressional Research Service, 1983).
8. U.S. Congress, Senate, *Congressional Record*, July 30, 1973, pp. S14174–83.
9. Cited in S. Rep. 93-220, p. 16.
10. U.S. Congress, Senate, Committee on Foreign Relations, *National Commitments*, 90th Cong., 1967, S. Rep. 797, p. 13 (hereafter cited as S. Rep. 90-797).
11. Senator Jacob Javits, *Who Makes War* (New York: William Morrow, 1973), p. 249.
12. Ibid., p. 254.
13. S. Rep. 90-797, p. 22

14. Javits, *Who Makes War*, p. 256.
15. U.S. Congress, Senate, Committee on Foreign Relations, *North Atlantic Treaty: Report on Executive Legislation*, 81st Cong., 1949, p. 8.
16. Javits, *Who Makes War*, p. 255.
17. S. Rep. 90-797, p. 18.
18. U.S. Congress, House, Committee on Foreign Affairs, *The War Powers Resolution*, John Sullivan (Washington, D.C.: Foreign Affairs Committee Print, 1982), p. 17 (hereafter cited as Sullivan, *War Powers Resolution*). Except as cited, factual information relating to the legislative history of the WPR is drawn chiefly from Sullivan's study.
19. U.S. Congress, Senate, *Congressional Record*, 91st Cong., June 25, 1969, p. S7132.
20. U.S. Congress, Senate, Committee on Foreign Relations, *National Commitments*, S. Rep. 129, 91st Cong., 1969, p. 26.
21. Ibid., p. 37.
22. Cited in S. Rep. 90-797, p. 4.
23. Ibid., pp. 23, 24.
24. Sullivan, *War Powers Resolution*, p. 23.
25. Ibid., pp. 37, 38.
26. Ibid., pp. 31–36.
27. Senator Thomas Eagleton, *War and Presidential Power* (New York: Liveright, 1974), p. 160.
28. U.S. Congress, House, *Congressional Record*, 93d Cong., May 10, 1973, p. H3598.
29. Sullivan, *War Powers Resolution*, p. 109.
30. Eagleton, *War and Presidential Powers*, p. 102.
31. U.S. Congress, House, *Congressional Record*, 93d Cong., June 29, 1973, p. H5663.
32. See, for example, Senator John Tower, "Congress vs. the President: The Formulation and Implementation of American Foreign Policy," *Foreign Affairs* (Winter 1981–82): 230–46.
33. Thomas Franck and Edward Weisband, *Foreign Policy by Congress* (New York: Oxford University Press, 1979), p. 25.
34. Sullivan, *War Powers Resolution*, p. 109.

CHAPTER 2: THE WAR POWERS RESOLUTION

1. U.S. Congress, House, Committee on Foreign Affairs, *The War Powers Resolution*, John Sullivan (Washington, D.C.: Foreign Affairs Committee Print, 1982), p. 67 (hereafter cited as Sullivan, *War Powers Resolution*).

2. U.S. Congress, Senate, Committee on Foreign Relations, *War Powers*, 92d Cong., 1972, S. Rep. 606, pp. 2, 3.
3. Senator Thomas Eagleton, *War and Presidential Power* (New York: Liveright, 1974), p. 190.
4. The two legislative vehicles differ in that a joint resolution is presented to the President for signature—and accordingly can be vetoed—whereas a concurrent resolution is not. The mechanism employed in the WPR, as well as in the laws cited below, came to be known as the "legislative veto." In theory, it consisted of a grant of power to the Executive branch subject to revocation in any particular case by concurrent resolution. As will be detailed below, both the legislative veto mechanism in general and its employment in the case of the WPR have been topics of ongoing controversy.
5. U.S. Congress, House, Committee on Foreign Affairs, *War Powers*, 93d Cong., 1973, H. Rep. 287, p. 13.
6. Eagleton, *War and Presidential Power*, p. 204.
7. Ibid., pp. 204, 205.
8. U.S. Congress, House, *Conference Report to Accompany H. J. Res. 542*, 93d Cong., 1973, H. Rep. 547, p. 14.
9. President Richard M. Nixon, "Veto Message on H. J. Res. 542," 93d Cong., 1973, House Document 171.
10. For a presentation of the political and legal case made by opponents of the WPR, see Robert F. Turner, *The War Powers Resolution in Theory and Practice* (Philadelphia: Foreign Policy Research Institute, 1983). An exhaustive analysis of legal arguments and precedents favorable to the congressional position can be found in Francis Wormuth and Edwin Firmage, *To Chain the Dog of War* (Dallas: Southern Methodist University Press, 1986).
11. U.S. Congress, Senate, Committee on Foreign Relations, *War Powers*, 93d Cong., 1973, S. Rep. 220, p. 21.

CHAPTER 3: REVOLUTION OR LOST OPPORTUNITIES?

1. The presidential reports submitted in these cases are printed in U.S. Congress, House, Committee on Foreign Affairs, *The War Powers Resolution: Relevant Documents, Correspondence, Reports* (Foreign Affairs Committee Print, 1983), pp. 40–49.
2. U.S. Library of Congress, Congressional Research Service, *The War Powers Resolution, A Decade of Experience*, Ellen Collier (Washington, D.C.: Congressional Research Service, 1984), pp. 15–20.

NOTES

3. U.S. Congress, House, Committee on Foreign Affairs, *War Powers, a Test of Compliance, Hearings before the Subcommittee on International Security and Scientific Affairs*, 94th Cong., May 7, June 4, 1974, pp. 94, 95 (hereafter cited as House, *War Powers, A Test of Compliance*).
4. Ibid., p. 97.
5. Ibid., p. 96.
6. U.S. Congress, Senate, Committee on Foreign Relations, *War Powers Resolution, Hearings before the Committee on Foreign Relations*, 95th Cong., July 13, 14, 15, 1977, pp. 208–12 (hereafter cited as Senate, *1977 Senate War Powers Hearings*).
7. House, *War Powers, A Test of Compliance*, pp. 9, 10.
8. U.S. Congress, House, Committee on Foreign Affairs, *War Powers*, 93d Cong., 1973, H. Rep. 287, p. 7 (hereafter cited as H. Rep. 93-287).
9. U.S. Congress, House, Committee on Foreign Affairs, *The War Powers Resolution*, John Sullivan (Washington, D.C.: Foreign Affairs Committee Print, 1982), p. 202 (hereafter cited as Sullivan, *War Powers Resolution*).
10. Ibid., pp. 229–36.
11. H. Rep. 93-287, p. 8.
12. U.S. Congress, House, Committee on International Relations, *Deaths of American Military Personnel in the Korean Demilitarized Zone, Hearings before the Subcommittee on International Political and Military Affairs and International Organizations*, 94th Cong., September 1, 1976, p. 16.
13. House, *War Powers, A Test of Compliance*, p. 3.
14. H. Rep. 93-287, pp. 6, 7.
15. U.S. Congress, Senate, Committee on Foreign Relations, *The Situation in Iran, Hearings before the Committee on Foreign Relations*, 96th Cong., May 8, 1980, p. 4.
16. House, *War Powers, A Test of Compliance*, p. 53.
17. Ibid., p. 55.
18. Sullivan, *War Powers Resolution*, pp. 183, 184.
19. S. Rep. 93-220, p. 27.
20. U.S. Congress, House, Committee on Foreign Affairs, *Congressional Oversight of War Powers Compliance: Zaire Airlift, Hearings before the Subcommittee on International Security and Scientific Affairs*, 95th Cong., August 20, 1978, pp. 6, 7 (Findley) and 17, 18 (Hansell).
21. This exchange of letters is printed in House, *War Powers Resolution: Relevant Documents, Correspondence, Reports*, pp. 37–39.
22. Thomas Franck and Edward Weisband, *Foreign Policy by Congress* (New York: Oxford University Press, 1979), p. 157.
23. See, for example, speech by President Gerald Ford of April 11, 1977, reprinted in Senate, *1977 War Powers Hearings*, pp. 325–31.
24. Senate, *1977 Senate War Powers Hearings*, p. 19.

25. Ibid., pp. 177–79.
26. Sullivan, *War Powers Resolution*, pp. 257, 258.
27. Factual information on this episode is drawn largely from U.S. Congress, House, Committee on Foreign Affairs, *Congressional-Executive Relations and the Turkish Arms Embargo*, Ellen Laipson (Washington, D.C.: Foreign Affairs Committee Print, 1981) (hereafter cited as Laipson, *Congressional-Executive Relations*).
28. Ibid., p. 19.
29. Much has been made of the impact of the "Greek Lobby" and of Greek-American Members of Congress in this affair. While there is little doubt that ethnic considerations were important to some key leaders of the embargo movement—Representative Paul Sarbanes (D-MD), for example—they were not important for others, such as Senator Eagleton. The impact of ethnic lobbying on Congress as a whole does not seem to have been the decisive factor in this issue. See ibid., p. 19, n.
30. Neil Livingston and Manfred Von Nordheim, "The United States Congress and the Angola Crisis," *Strategic Review* (Spring 1977): 37.
31. Franck and Weisband, *Foreign Policy*, pp. 47, 48.
32. Laipson, *Congressional-Executive Relations*, pp. 24–26.
33. It should be noted that the Executive branch never sought to employ the mechanism set out in the Clark Amendment, instead seeking total repeal of legislative restrictions on policy toward Angola—an effort in which the Reagan Administration was finally successful in 1985. The Clark Amendment's importance as a legislative model, however, remains.
34. For a detailed description of the growth of congressional staff and support services, and an analysis of its significance, see Franck and Weisband, *Foreign Policy*, pp. 227–53.
35. U.S. Congress, Senate, *Congressional Record*, 96th Cong., July 1, 1980, p. S9092.

CHAPTER 4: PRESIDENTIAL INITIATIVES

1. The text of the presidential reports in the first six cases are printed in U.S. Congress, House, Committee on Foreign Affairs, *War Powers Resolution: Relevant Documents, Correspondence, Reports* (Foreign Affairs Committee Print, 1983), pp. 57–66, 84, 85. The President's report on the 1986 air raid against Libya was printed in *Weekly Compilation of Presidential Documents* 22, no. 16 (April 22, 1986): 499, 500; the report on Persian Gulf operations was printed in U.S. Congress, Senate, *Congressional Record*, 100th Cong., October 21, 1987, pp. S14654, S14655.

2. *Immigration and Naturalization Service* vs. *Chadha*, 103 Ct. 2764 (1983).
3. U.S. Congress, House, Committee on Foreign Affairs, *Congress and Foreign Policy, 1983*, ed. Ellen Collier (Washington, D.C.: Foreign Affairs Committee Print, 1984), p. 135 (hereafter cited as Collier, *Congress and Foreign Policy, 1983*).
4. *U.S. Senate* vs. *Federal Trade Commission*, 103 Ct. 3556 (1983).
5. Collier, *Congress and Foreign Policy, 1983*, p. 138.
6. U.S. Library of Congress, Congressional Research Service, *The War Powers Resolution: A Decade of Experience*, Ellen Collier (Washington, D.C.: Congressional Research Service, 1984), p. 22.
7. *Washington Post*, 19 December 1987, p. A11.
8. U.S. Congress, Senate, Committee on Foreign Relations, *Nomination of Alexander Haig, Hearings before the Committee on Foreign Relations*, 97th Cong., January 9, 10, 12, 13, 15, 1981, p. 40.
9. Ibid.
10. Speech by Secretary of Defence Caspar Weinberger to the National Press Club on 28 November 1984, printed in *New York Times*, 29 November 1984, p. A5.
11. U.S. Congress, Senate, Committee on Foreign Relations, *Nomination of George Shultz, Hearings before the Committee on Foreign Relations*, 97th Cong., July 13, 14, 1982, p. 113.
12. *New York Times*, 26 March 1983, pp. 1, 7.
13. For a chronology of U.S. decision-making leading up to the invasion, see "The Making of an Invasion," *Washington Post*, 30 October 1983, pp. 1, 14, 15.
14. *Washington Post*, 29 October 1983, pp. 1, 10.
15. U.S. Congress, Senate, *Congressional Record*, 98th Cong., October 26, 1983, p. S14610.
16. Cited by Michael Rubner, "The Reagan Administration, the 1973 War Powers Resolution, and the Invasion of Grenada," *Political Science Quarterly* (Winter 1985–86): 629.
17. U.S. Congress, Senate, Committee on Foreign Relations, *The Invasion of Grenada, Hearings before the Committee on Foreign Relations*, 98th Cong., October 27, 1983, p. 11 (hereafter cited as Senate, *The Invasion of Grenada*).
18. *Washington Post*, 24 October 1983, p. A4.
19. Ibid., 30 October 1986, p. 14.
20. Cited by Rubner, "The Reagan Administration," pp. 633, 634.
21. Ed Magnuson, "Now Make It Work," *Time*, November 14, 1983, p. 23.
22. Senate, *The Invasion of Grenada*, p. 12.
23. U.S. Congress, House, Committee on Foreign Affairs, *U.S. Military Activities in Grenada: Implications for U.S. Policy in the Eastern Caribbean, Hearings before the Subcommittees on International Security and Scientific*

Affairs and on Western Hemisphere Affairs, 98th Cong., October 29, 1983, p. 15 (hereafter cited as House, *U.S. Military Activities in Grenada*).
24. U.S. Congress, House, Committee on Foreign Affairs, *Grenada War Powers: Full Compliance, Reporting, and Implementation, Hearings before the Committee on Foreign Affairs*, 98th Cong., October 27, 1983.
25. U.S. Congress, Senate, *Congressional Record*, 98th Cong., October 28, 1983, pp. S14868 et seq.
26. Ibid., p. S14871.
27. U.S. Congress, Senate, *Congressional Record*, 98th Cong., November 17, 1983, p. S16593.
28. House, *U.S. Military Actions in Grenada*, pp. 18, 19.
29. *New York Times*, 28 December 1985, pp. 1, 4.
30. Ibid., 25 March 1986, pp. 1, A11; 26 March 1986, pp. 1, A8.
31. Printed in U.S. Congress, House, Committee on Foreign Affairs, *War Powers, Libya, and State-Sponsored Terrorism, Hearings before the Subcommittee on Arms Control, International Security and Science*, 99th Cong., April 29, 1986, p. 208 (hereafter cited as House, *War Powers, Libya, and State-Sponsored Terrorism*).
32. *Weekly Compilation of Presidential Documents* 22, no. 13 (March 31, 1986): 423.
33. House, *War Powers, Libya, and State-Sponsored Terrorism*, p. 209.
34. *New York Times*, 15 May 1986, pp. 1, A10.
35. U.S. Congress, House, *Congressional Record*, 99th Cong., April 16, 1986, p. H1924.
36. House, *War Powers, Libya, and State-Sponsored Terrorism*, p. 37.
37. Ibid.
38. U.S. Congress, Senate, *Congressional Record*, 99th Cong., May 17, 1986, p. S4423.
39. House, *War Powers, Libya, and State-Sponsored Terrorism*, p. 28.
40. See, for example, "Unshackle the Commander," *Wall Street Journal*, 9 September 1986.
41. U.S. Congress, Senate, Committee on Foreign Relations, *U.S. Policy in the Western Hemisphere*, 97th Cong., 1982. S. Rep. 470, p. 4.
42. U.S. Congress, House, Committee on Foreign Affairs, *Congress and Foreign Policy*, 1981, ed. Ellen Collier (Washington, D.C.: Foreign Affairs Committee Print, 1982), p. 122.
43. U.S. Congress, House, 97th Cong., *Congressional Record*, March 5, 1981, p. E901.
44. House, *War Powers Resolution: Relevant Documents*, p. 52.
45. U.S. Congress, House, Committee on Foreign Affairs, *Congress and Foreign Policy*, 1982, ed. Ellen Collier (Washington, D.C.: Foreign Affairs Committee Print, 1983), p. 71 (hereafter cited as Collier, *Congress and Foreign Policy, 1982*).

46. U.S. Congress, Senate, Committee on Foreign Relations, *Situation in El Salvador, Hearings before the Committee on Foreign Relations*, 97th Cong., March 18, 1982, p. 23.
47. Ibid. pp. 29–31.
48. United States General Accounting Office, *Applicability of Certain U.S. Laws that Pertain to U.S. Military Involvement in El Salvador* (id. 82-53), June 27, 1982.
49. U.S. Congress, Senate, Committee on Foreign Relations, *U.S. Policy in Central America, Hearings before the Committee on Foreign Relations*, 97th Congress, May 4, 1982.
50. Ibid., p. 189.
51. Ibid., p. 190.
52. U.S. Congress, Senate, *Congressional Record*, 97th Cong., April 14, 1982, p. S3469. The text of Symm's resolution was printed in Senate, *U.S. Policy in Central America*.
53. U.S. Congress, Senate, *Congressional Record*, 97th Cong., August 11, 1982, p. S10157.
54. S. Rep. 97-470, p. 4.
55. Ibid., p. 7.
56. U.S. Congress, Senate, *Congressional Record*, 97th Cong., August 11, 1982, pp. S10155–S10168.
57. Ibid., p. S10233.
58. See, for example, the "War Powers in Central America Act" (S. 1692, 98th Cong.) introduced by Senator Gary Hart, which would have permitted an increase in U.S. military involvement in Central America only following a Joint Resolution of Congress authorizing such a move, or pursuant to a written report by the President stating that such a move was necessary to protect Americans or to respond to a threat of attack against the United States. U.S. Congress, Senate, *Congressional Record*, 98th Cong., July 27, 1983, pp. S11014, S11015.
59. *New York Times*, March 30, 1984, pp. 1, A4.
60. See U.S. Congress, House, Committee on Foreign Affairs, *Nicaraguan Incursions into Honduras, Hearings before the Subcommittee on Western Hemisphere Affairs*, 99th Cong., April 8, 1986, pp. 15–17.
61. U.S. Library of Congress, Congressional Research Service, unpublished data, 1986.
62. Collier, *Congress and Foreign Policy, 1982*, pp. 85, 86.
63. U.S. Congress, House, *Conference Report to Accompany S. 2586*, H. Rep. 880, 97th Cong., 1982, p. 45.
64. Collier, *Congress and Foreign Policy, 1983*, p. 47.
65. U.S. Congress, House, Committee on Foreign Affairs, *Congress and Foreign Policy*, 1984, ed. Ellen Collier (Washington, D.C.: Foreign Affairs Committee Print, 1985), p. 37.

66. Appendix to Comptroller General's Decision B213137, June 22, 1984. Cited in ibid., p. 40.
67. *New York Times*, 13 July 1986.
68. U.S. Congress, House, Committee on Appropriations, *Military Construction Appropriation for 1987, Hearings before the Subcommittee on Military Construction Appropriations*, pt. 5, 99th Cong., March 12, 1986, pp. 363, 364.
69. U.S. Congress, House, *Congressional Record*, 98th Cong., May 23, 1984, p. H4745.
70. Ibid., June 18, 1984, p. S7498; April 4, 1984, p. S3758.

CHAPTER 5: CONGRESS DEFENDS ITS GAINS

1. *New York Times*, 20 August 1982, pp. 1, A13. See also chronology of the Israeli invasion and subsequent events, ibid., p. A12.
2. Ibid., 11 September 1982, p. 5.
3. Ibid., 14 September 1982, sec. 4, p. 1.
4. Ibid., 22 September 1982, p. A22. For the text of President Reagan's announcement, see ibid., 21 September 1982, p. A17. The text of the U.S.-Lebanese agreement is printed in U.S. Congress, House, Committee on Foreign Affairs, *War Powers Resolution: Relevant Documents, Correspondence, Reports* (Foreign Affairs Committee Print, 1983), pp. 74–76.
5. Text of the Israeli-Lebanese Agreement is printed in *New York Times*, 17 May 1983, p. A12.
6. Ibid., 15 May 1983, p. 8.
7. Ibid., 30 August 1983, pp. 1, A8.
8. Michael D. Malone, William H. Miller, and Joseph W. Robben, "From Presence to American Intervention," *Survival*, September–October 1986, p. 432.
9. *New York Times*, 8 February 1984, p. A9.
10. Ibid., 7 July 1982, pp. 7, A4; 14 July 1982, p. A8.
11. *Congressional Quarterly Weekly Report*, July 17, 1982, p. 1695 (hereafter cited as *Congressional Quarterly*).
12. Speaking during the confirmation hearings for Secretary of State-designate George Shultz, for example, Senator Percy stated, "I have expressed my personal judgment that it would be best to act pursuant to Section 4(a)(1)." U.S. Congress, Senate, Committee on Foreign Relations, *Nomination of George Shultz, Hearings before the Committee on Foreign Relations*, 97th Cong., 1982, p. 14.
13. *Congressional Quarterly*, July 17, 1982, p. 1695.
14. House, *War Powers Resolution: Relevant Documents*, pp. 60, 61.
15. *Congressional Quarterly*, October 21, 1982, p. 2469.

16. The relevant sections of the LEEA are printed in House, *War Powers: Relevant Documents*, p. 77.
17. U.S. Congress, House, Committee on Foreign Affairs, *Congress and Foreign Policy, 1983*, ed. Ellen Collier (Washington, D.C.: Foreign Affairs Committee Print, 1984), p. 11 (hereafter cited as Collier, *Congress and Foreign Policy, 1983*).
18. *Congressional Quarterly*, September 3, 1983, p. 1876; September 17, 1983, p. 1923.
19. Printed in House, *War Powers: Relevant Documents*, pp. 78–81.
20. U.S. Congress, Senate, Committee on Foreign Affairs, *Multinational Force in Lebanon*, 98th Cong., 1983, S. Rep. 242, p. 16.
21. Ibid.
22. U.S. Congress, Senate, Committee on Foreign Relations, *War Powers Resolution, Hearings before the Committee on Foreign Relations*, 98th Cong., September 21, 1983, p. 28 (hereafter cited as Senate, *Lebanon War Powers Hearings*).
23. The full text of President Reagan's letter is printed in *Congressional Quarterly*, October 1, 1983, p. 2044.
24. U.S. Congress, House, Committee on Foreign Affairs, *Statutory Authorization Under the War Powers Resolution—Lebanon, Hearings before the Committee on Foreign Relations*, 98th Cong., September 21, 22, 1983, p. 60.
25. Ibid., pp. 63, 73.
26. It should also be noted that the MFLR provided a vehicle for Members who—overtly or implicitly—supported deployment of the MNF in the context of U.S. cooperation with Israel, but who wished to register support for the WPR, a vehicle by which both of these goals could be furthered.
27. Collier, *Congress and Foreign Policy, 1983*, p. 20.
28. Ibid.
29. U.S. Congress, Senate, *Congressional Record*, 98th Cong., September 29, 1983, p. S13164.
30. Senate, *Lebanon War Powers Resolution Hearings*, September 21, 1983, p. 2.
31. U.S. Congress, House, Committee on Foreign Affairs, *Congress and Foreign Policy, 1984*, ed. Ellen Collier (Washington, D.C.: Foreign Affairs Committee Print, 1985), p. 13.
32. *Congressional Quarterly*, January 7, 1984, p. 3.
33. U.S. Congress, House, Committee on Foreign Affairs, *The Crisis in Lebanon, Hearings before the Committee on Foreign Affairs*, 98th Cong., February 1, 2, 1984, pp. 27–33.
34. William E. Smith, "Looking to Washington," *Time*, November 1, 1984, pp. 44–46.

35. Malone, Miller, and Robben, "From Presence to Intervention," p. 423.
36. *Congressional Quarterly*, April 20, 1985, p. 710.
37. U.S. Congress, House, *Congressional Record*, 98th Cong., April 27, 1983, p. H2416.
38. U.S. Congress, House, Committee on Intelligence, *Amendment to the Intelligence Authorization Act for Fiscal Year 1983*, 98th Cong., 1983, H. Rep. 122, part 1, p. 19.
39. Ibid., pp. 11, 12.
40. Ibid., p. 11.
41. U.S. Congress, House, *Congressional Record*, 98th Cong., July 28, 1983, p. H5881.
42. U.S. Congress, House, *Intelligence Authorization for Fiscal 1984; Conference Report to Accompany H.R. 2968*, 98th Cong., 1983, H. Rep. 569, p. 3.
43. *Congressional Quarterly*, April 7, 1984, p. 768.
44. Ibid., April 14, 1984, p. 833.
45. U.S. Congress, Senate, *Congressional Record*, 98th Cong., June 18, 1984, p. S7517.
46. Ibid., June 25, 1984, p. S8150
47. U.S. Congress, House, *Congressional Record*, 99th Cong., June 12, 1985, p. H4169, H4170.
48. Ibid., June 25, 1986, p. H14278.
49. Ibid., pp. H14253–H14256.

CHAPTER 6: THE COLLECTIVE JUDGMENT OF CONGRESS AND THE PRESIDENT

1. *New York Times*, 18 May 1987, pp. 1, A12; 21 May 1987, p. A18.
2. Ibid., 20 May 1987, p. A20.
3. U.S. Congress, Senate, *Congressional Record*, 100th Cong., May 21, 1987, p. S6953.
4. Ibid., p. S6952.
5. *New York Times*, 29 May 1987, pp. 1, A11.
6. See, for example, the President's statement of 29 May 1987, printed in *New York Times*, 30 May 1987, p. 6.
7. U.S. Congress, House, *Congressional Record*, July 8, 1987, p. H6106.
8. Ibid., p. H6090.
9. Ibid., p. H6104.
10. U.S. Congress, Senate, *Congressional Record*, 100th Cong., July 15, 1987, p. S9937.

11. For details of these incidents, see *New York Times*, 25 July 1987, p. 1; 22 September 1987, pp. 1, A6; 9 October 1987, pp. 1, A6.
12. President Reagan's report is printed in U.S. Congress, Senate, *Congressional Record*, October 21, 1987, pp. S14654, 14655.
13. See *New York Times*, 6 August 1987, pp. 1, A15.
14. Ibid., 8 August 1987, pp. 1, 4.
15. See, for example, President Reagan's speech to the Organization of American States of 7 October 1987, printed in *New York Times*, 8 October 1987, p. A12.
16. Ibid., 8 August 1987, p. 4.
17. *Congressional Quarterly Weekly Report*, November 14, 1987, pp. 2789–91.
18. Ibid., p. 2790.
19. Enforcing such a funding cutoff is, of course, not as easy as legislating it. Ironically, however, the Iran-Contra affair stands as testimony to the effectiveness of congressional budget controls. The irregular, and ultimately self-defeating, methods to which the principals in that operation resorted to obtain funds demonstrates the difficulty of challenging a congressional ban while acting within the system.
20. Certain more distant examples, such as the congressional role in the Spanish-American War of 1898, suggest that congressional majorities can also force aggressive policies on a reluctant Executive. Even if this example were relevant in the very different political and strategic environment of the late twentieth century, however, it hardly stands as an example of an ideal foreign policy.
21. For an empirical exploration of this topic, see Richard J. Stoll, "The Sound of the Guns!" *American Political Science Quarterly* (April 1987): 223–37. Based on a statistical analysis of key congressional votes, Stoll concludes that the likelihood of the President winning an important vote on a foreign policy question rises significantly in the thirty days immediately following the initiation of U.S. military action.
22. U.S. Congress, Senate, Committee on Foreign Relations, *War Powers Resolution, Hearings before the Committee on Foreign Relations*, 95th Cong., 1977, pp. 2–15 and 338–51. The arguments in favor of such a measure are presented in Michael J. Glennon, "Strengthening the War Powers Resolution, the Case for Purse-String Restrictions," *Minnesota Law Review* 60, no. 1 (November 1975).
23. U.S. Congress, House, Committee on Foreign Affairs, *The War Powers Resolution*, ed. John Sullivan (Washington, D.C.: Foreign Affairs Committee Print, 1982), pp. 273–275. See also pp. 42–43 above.
24. Byrd's resolution is printed in U.S. Congress, House, Committee on Foreign Affairs, *War Powers, Libya, and State Sponsored Terrorism, Hearings before the Subcommittee on Arms Control, International Security and Science*, 99th Cong., 1986, pp. 216, 217. The Members designated by this

measure are the Speaker and President Pro Tem., the Majority and Minority Leaders of the two Houses, and the chairman and ranking minority member of the House and Senate Armed Services, Intelligence, and Foreign Affairs/Relations Committees. For a more extensive discussion of the merits of this proposal, see also the statement of former Assistant Secretary of State J. Brian Atwood, ibid., pp. 83–86.

INDEX

Advisors: in El Salvador, 81–83, 89, 90;
  in Vietnam, 40, 44
Alternative policies, necessity for successful opposition, 139
Angola, xii, 52, 54–56, 58, 118, 150
Arias, Oscar, 135
Arms Export Control Act (1976), 57, 58
Arms sales, xiii, 51, 57, 58
Articles of Confederation, 6
Aspin, Congressman Les (D–WI), 113
Austin, Hudson, 70

Baker, Howard, 72, 102, 106, 116
Barbados, 70, 71, 72
Beirut
  U.S. Marines in, xiii–xiv, 64, 75, 97–117, 138, 139, 145
  see also Lebanon
Bell, William, III, 77
Benghazi, air strike against, 64, 69, 76
Bentsen, Senator Lloyd (D–TX), 25, 106, 122–123
Berlin, 9
  discotheque bombing, 78
Biden, Senator Joseph (D–DE), 83, 123
Bingham, Congressman Jonathan (D–NY), 20, 23, 27, 47

Bishop, Maurice, 70
Boland, Congressman Edward (D–MA), 118, 123
  Amendments, 118–121, 124, 125, 126
Broomfield, Congressman William (R–MI), 78, 82
Budgetary reform, 145–146
Burger, Warren, 66
Bush, George, 70–71
Byrd, Senator Robert (D–WV), 4–5, 66–67, 72, 75, 78
  amendment to War Powers Resolution, 83–87, 93, 94
  and Persian Gulf, 132–133
  and standing consultative committee, 149

Cambodia, 13, 14, 15, 16, 23
  evacuation of, 32, 38, 42, 43
  reconnaissance flights, 32, 39
Campbell, Congressman Caroll, Jr. (R–SC), 94
Caribbean Common Market, 72
Carter, Jimmy
  and Iranian hostages, 150
  and Turkish arms embargo, 56
  and War Powers Resolution, 31–32, 35, 37, 38, 39–40, 41–42, 44, 45, 47–48, 59, 69, 87
  and Zaire airlift, 39–40

INDEX

Case, Senator Clifford (R–NJ), 49–50
Casey, William, 122
Casualties, number of and congressional response, 137–138
Central America, *see* El Salvador; Honduras; Nicaragua
Chad, 64
China, 8
Chouf Mountains, 100, 116
Christopher, Warren, 42
Church, Senator Frank (D–ID), 14, 21, 28, 49–50
CIA, 23, 122, 125
Clark, Senator Dick (D–IA), 54–55, 56–57
  Amendment, 55, 58
Cohen, Senator William (R–ME), 121, 123
Combat equipment and War Powers Resolution, 82–83, 88, 91, 101
Concurrent resolution, 23–24, 27, 36, 66–67, 111–112
Congressional Budget Office, 57
Congressional Research Service, 7, 57
Conservatives and War Powers Resolution, 12, 16, 21–22, 23, 131, 132
Consultation provisions of War Powers Resolution, 20, 26–27, 41–43, 58, 80, 147–150
  and El Salvador, 86
  enforcement problems, 49, 50
  executive branch response, 46, 48
  and Grenada, 71–73, 78
  and Lebanon, 101
  and Libya, 77, 78–80
  and Persian Gulf, 129
  and security, 149
  and standing committee, 148–150
Contingency funds, 146
Contras, 117–126, 134, 138
  see also Iran-Contra affair; Nicaragua
Coolidge, Calvin, 8
Cooper, Senator John Sherman (D–KY), 14, 21, 28, 49
Costa Rica, 119
Cotton, Senator Norris (R–NH), 17
Covert operations, xi–xii, 49, 59, 137
  and Angola, 54–55
  and Nicaragua, 89–90, 119

Crockett, Congressman George (D–MI), 67
Cuba: crisis, 9
  and El Salvador, 84–85, 119
  and Grenada, 70, 72–73, 75
  Cuba Resolution, 84–85
Cyprus, 52–54, 55–56, 59

Dam, Kenneth, 72–73, 75
Danang sealift, 32, 38, 42, 43
Davis, Nathaniel, 54
Deadline for actions, *see* Time limit on presidential military initiatives
Defense Authorization Bill, 93–96
Dole, Senator Robert (R–KS), 25, 78, 79, 130, 131
Dominican Republic, 141
Dominick, Congressman Peter (R–CO), 12
Duarte, Jose Napoleon, 88
Durenberger, Senator David (R–MN), 121

Eagleberger, Lawrence, 113
Eagleton, Senator Thomas (D–MO), 15, 16, 21–22, 23, 24–25, 28, 34, 43, 53, 82, 143, 144, 147
East, Senator John (R–NC), 86
Eisenhower, Dwight D., 9
  doctrine, 10
El Salvador, 67, 81–88, 90, 121, 139
  Arias plan, 135
  and Nicaraguan arms, 118, 119, 124
Emergency Price Control Act, 24
Enlargement of military forces and War Powers Resolution, 38, 40
  and Honduras, 88, 91
  and Lebanon, 104
Ervin, Senator Sam (D–NC), 13
Executive Reorganization Act, 24

Fairbanks, Richard, 82
Fascell, Congressman Dante (D–FL), 77, 90, 93, 130–131
Findley, Congressman Paul (R–IL), 20, 27, 39–40, 45, 46
Florida, expedition to (1816–1817), 8
Foley, Congressman Thomas (D–WA), 93–95, 96, 123
Ford, Gerald, 15, 16

and Angola, 54–55
and Turkish arms embargo, 52–54
and War Powers Resolution, 31–32, 35, 36, 38, 39, 40, 41–42, 43, 44–47, 48–50, 59, 69, 71, 87
Foreign Assistance Act (1974), 51
Formosa, 9, 10
France, 98
F.T.C. case, 66
Fulbright, Senator William (D–AR), 23, 49

Gemayel, Amin, 115
Gemayel, Bashir, 98
General Accounting Office, 57, 83, 92
Gerry, Elbridge, 6
Glenn, Senator John (D–OH), 83
Goldwater, Senator Barry (R–AZ), 7, 22, 25, 26, 74, 86, 109
and mining of Nicaraguan harbors, 122
Graves, General Ernest, 83
Greece, 52–54
Green, Judge Joyce, 67
Grenada invasion, xi, 64, 69–76, 78, 79–81, 95–96, 115, 137, 146, 147
and consultation with Congress, 71–73, 78
Gruening, Senator Ernest (D–AK), 9
Guatemala, 135, 139
Gulf of Sidra, 76
Gulf of Tonkin Resolution, 9–11, 14, 24, 29, 86
repeal, 13, 21

Haig, Alexander, 68
Hamilton, Alexander, 6–7
Hamilton, Congressman Lee (D–IN), 109, 113
Hansell, Herbert, 37
Hart, Senator Gary (D–CO), 74–75
Hatfield, Senator Mark (R–OR), 4, 14, 94, 132
Headquarters operations, 28
Helms, Senator Jesse (R–NC), 85
Honduras, 87–90, 96, 121, 139
military exercises, 90–93, 123
and Nicaraguan arms, 119
Hoover, Herbert, 8
Hostilities, definition of, 38–39

and El Salvador, 83
and Grenada, 73
and Lebanon, 101–102, 103, 106
and Persian Gulf, 132
Huddleston, Senator Walter (D–KY), 122–123
Hughes–Ryan Amendment, 51, 57
Hunter, Congressman Duncan (R–CA), 94

Immigration and Naturalization Act, 66
Inouye, Senator Daniel (D–HI), 122–123
INS vs. *Chaddah*, 65–66
Intelligence activities
congressional oversight of, xiii, 23, 57, 58
Intelligence Authorization Act, 118, 119, 120, 123
Intelligence Oversight Act (1980), 57, 58
Iran
hostage rescue attempt, 32, 38, 42, 43, 150
and Persian Gulf forces, xi, 129, 130, 131–132
Iran–Contra affair, 126, 134
Iraq, xi, 129
Isolationism in Congress, 142
Israel, 64
and Lebanon, 98, 99, 100, 102, 103, 115, 116
Italy, 98

Jackson, Justice Robert H., 7, 9
Jackson State massacres, 13
Jamaica, 71
Javits, Senator Jacob (R–NY), 8–9, 21–22, 23, 25, 27, 38, 47, 59, 111
Jefferson, Thomas, 7
Johnson, Lyndon B., 9, 11, 64, 127
Joint Committee on National Security, 42, 148
Joint resolutions, 24, 66–67, 106, 111–112, 114

Kennedy, Senator Edward (D–MA), 94
Kennedy, John F., 9, 40
Kent State massacre, 13

INDEX

Kissinger, Henry, 52–54, 56
Korean DMZ, tree–cutting incident, 32, 40
Korean War, 7, 8–9, 29, 127
Kuwait, 129, 133, 134
Laos, 14, 15, 23, 44
Leahy, Senator Patrick (D–VT), 94, 123
Lebanese Armed Forces (LAF), 99–100, 107
Lebanon, xii, 9, 104, 105, 106, 108, 110
   and consultation with Congress, 101
   and Reagan administration, 65, 75, 97–117, 129, 137–138, 141
   see also Beirut
Lebanon Emergency Assistance Act (LEAA), 103–104, 108, 114, 116, 139
Leigh, Monroe, 36, 38, 39, 43
Lend-Lease Act, 24
Libya, 64, 69, 76–81, 95–96, 115, 137, 138, 147
   and consultation with Congress, 77, 78–80
Lowry, Congressman Mike (D–WA), 130–131

McDonald, General Wesley, 72–73
McGee, Senator Gale (D–WY), 22, 26
McGovern, Senator George (D–SD), 14
Madison, James, 6–7
Mansfield, Senator Mike, (D–MT), 12
Mayaguez incident, 32, 36, 38, 42–43, 71, 75–76
Mexican War, 7
Middle East Resolution, 9, 10–11, 24
Military Construction Authorization Bill, 92, 125
Morse, Senator Wayne (D–OR), 9
Movement of foreign troops and War Powers Resolution, 32, 39–40, 45, 69, 88–89
Moynihan, Senator Daniel Patrick (D–NY), 121, 122–123
Multinational Force and Observers:
   and Beirut, 97–117
   and Sinai, 64, 68, 102
Multination Force in Lebanon Resolution (MFLR), 106–111, 114

National Commitments Resolution, 11–12, 19, 21, 22, 127
National Security Council, 126
NATO treaty, 10, 28, 52
Nelson-Bingham Amendment, 51, 57
Neutrality Proclamation of 1793, 6–7
New Jewel Movement, 70
Nicaragua, xi–xii, xiii–xiv, 58, 150
   and Contra aid, 117–126, 134, 138
   and El Salvador, 118, 119, 124
   and Honduras, 88–90, 91
   and mining of ports, 122–124, 134, 138
Nixon, Richard M., xii, 11–12, 13, 14–17
   and War Powers Resolution, 20, 22, 25–26, 28, 35, 46–47, 64, 110
NORAD, 28

Obando y Bravo, Miguel, 135–136
Obey, Congressman David (D–WI), 110
O'Neill, Congressman Tip (D–MA), 72, 78, 89
   and Lebanon, 106, 109–110, 113
Ottinger, Congressman Richard (D–NY), 82
Oversight and War Powers Resolution, 27, 34–37, 43–44, 58, 143
   enforcement problems, 49
   executive branch response, 46, 47, 68
   and Honduras, 92
   and intelligence activities, xiii, 23, 57, 58

Palestine Liberation Organization (PLO), 98
Palmerola Air Force Base, Honduras, 88
Pell, Senator Claiborne (D–RI), 25, 78
Percy, Senator Charles (R–IL), 85–86, 102, 106, 111
Pershing, General John J., 8
Persian Gulf
   and consultation with Congress, 129
   F-15s to, 48
   and Soviet Union, 129, 130
   U.S. naval forces in, 3–5, 64, 128–134, 136–137, 141, 145
Phnom Penh, evacuation of, 32, 38, 42, 43

Point Salines Airport, 70
Political support for presidential actions, xii, 58–59, 80, 138
President, 142–143
  as commander-in-chief, 6–7, 9, 22, 24–25, 47, 84, 94, 128–134, 140–141 142, 147
  emergency response by, 46
  enumeration of powers under War Powers Resolution, 22, 24–25, 26, 33–34, 49, 143
  persuasiveness of, 95–96
  see also under individual presidents
Purse string power of Congress, xii, 14–17, 28–29, 51–52, 56–57, 139
  automatic cutoff deadline, 144–147
  and budgetary reform, 145–146
  and Central America, 90–95
  and Lebanon, 105, 110, 117, 139
  and previously appropriated funds, 139–140

Qadhafi, Muammar al-, 76–80

Reagan, Ronald, xiii
  and El Salvador, 81–88, 89, 90, 121, 139
  foreign policy, 63–65
  and Grenada, xi, 64, 69–76, 78, 79–81, 95–96, 115, 137, 146, 147
  and Honduras, 87–93, 96, 121, 123, 139
  and Lebanon, 65, 75, 97–111, 129, 137–138, 141
  and Libya, 64, 69, 76–81, 95–96, 115, 137, 138, 147
  and Nicaragua, 117–126, 134, 138
  and Persian Gulf, 4, 64, 126–134, 136–137, 141
  and War Powers Resolution, 4, 64–65, 67–68
Reporting requirements of War Powers Resolution, 20, 22, 27, 37–41, 145–146
  and El Salvador, 82
  executive branch response, 46–47
  and Lebanon, 106–107
  and Persian Gulf, 130, 132–133
Rescue of U.S. citizens abroad, 33–34, 76, 147
Rome airport bombing, 76–77
Roosevelt, Franklin D., xii

Roosevelt, Theodore, 8
Russell, Senator Richard (D–GA), 12

Saigon evacuation, 32, 38, 42, 43
Sarbanes, Senator Paul (D–MD), 74, 108
SEATO treaty, 10, 11
Security breaches, 79, 149
Seiberling, Congressman John (D–OH), 42–43
Shultz, George, 68, 70–71, 108, 136
Sinai, 64–68, 102
Sofaer, Abraham, 79
Solarz, Congressman Stephen (D–NY), 36–37, 109, 144
Soviet Union, 70, 76, 113
  and Persian Gulf, 129, 130
Spanish-American War, 7
Sparkman, Senator John (D–AL), 49
Standing consultative committee, 148–150
Stark, xi, 129, 132, 141
Steel industry seizure (1952), 7
Stennis, Senator John (D–MS), 12, 13, 21–22, 23, 25, 29
Studds, Congressman Gerry (D–MA), 75
Symms, Senator Steve (R–ID), 74
  Amendment, 84–86, 96
Syria, 99, 100, 113, 115

Taft, Senator Robert (R–IL), 25
Taft, William H., 8
Task Force Bravo, 88
Terrorism, actions against, 76–80, 138
  see also Libya
Time limit on presidential military initiatives, 21, 22, 23, 24–25, 27, 36, 43–44, 80, 143–146
  and Grenada, 72, 75
  and Lebanon, 103, 108–109
  and Persian Gulf, 132
Tonkin Gulf Resolution, *see* Gulf of Tonkin Resolution
Tower, Senator John (R–TX), 25, 59
Tripoli, air strikes against, 64, 69, 76, 138
Truman, Harry S, 7, 8, 9, 127
Tunney, Senator John (D–CA), 55, 58
Turkish arms embargo, 52–54, 55–56, 59, 118, 150

INDEX

Unarmed forces and War Powers Resolution, 39–40
United Nations Charter, Article 51, 78
U.S. Congress, House of Representatives
   Appropriations Committee, 90, 92, 93, 105
   Armed Services Committee, 90, 92, 149
   Foreign Affairs Committee, 19, 36–37, 39–40, 46, 74, 82, 83, 88–90, 93, 110
   Intelligence Committee, 58, 118, 121, 149
   and Vietnam War, 15
   and War Powers Resolution, 19–21, 22, 23–24, 25
U.S. Congress, Senate
   Foreign Relations Committee, 10, 11, 19, 23, 46, 68, 74, 80, 82, 83–84, 85, 94, 107, 149
   Intelligence Committee, 58, 130, 121, 122–123, 149
   and Vietnam War, 9–17
   and War Powers Resolution, 21–22, 23, 24–25
U.S. Constitution, 5–8, 12, 34–37
U.S. State Department
   and El Salvador, 82
   and Grenada, 73
   and Korean War, 8–9
   and Lebanon, 102
   and Libya, 78–79
   and War Powers Resolution, 36, 37, 38, 68
U.S. Supreme Court, 65–66

Vienna airport bombing, 77
Vietnam War, 9, 40, 127, 141
   advisors, introduction of, 40, 44
   legacy of, xiii, 5, 28, 54, 81–82, 84, 147
   U.S. Congress and, 9–17

War of 1812, 7
War Powers Resolution, xii, 4–5, 19–29

   and congressional restraint, 48–50
   early record of implementation, 37–45
   executive branch strategies, 45–48
   future directions, 140–142
   imprecision of language, 49
   initial proposals, 19–22
   legal issues, 65–67
   provisions, 26–28
   section 2a, 40
   section 2b, 35
   section 2c, 26, 33–34, 143
   section 3, 26–27, 41–43, 71–72, 73
   section 4a, 27, 37–41, 43, 68, 71, 73–74, 75, 88, 91, 101–102, 146
   section 5a, 27
   section 5b, 27, 43–44, 73, 110, 143–145
   section 5c, 27, 66–67
   section 6, 27
   section 7a, 27, 114
   section 8, 27–28
   section 8c, 44–45
   section 8d, 35
Warner, Senator John (R–VA), 132–133
Washington, George, 6
Weicker, Senator Lowell (R–CO), 4, 74, 132
Weinberger, Caspar, 68
Weiss, Congressman Ted (D–NY), 109
Who Makes War (Javits), 8–9
Wilson, Senator Pete (R–CA), 74
Wilson, Woodrow, 8
Wright, Congressman James (D–TX), 72, 78, 135–136

Zablocki, Congressman Clement (D–WI), 20–21, 22, 23–24, 27, 39 42, 43, 46, 47, 59, 82, 143, 148
   death, 89–90
   and Lebanon, 102, 109–110, 111
   and Nicaragua, 119
Zaire airlift, 32, 39–40, 45, 69

ABOUT THE AUTHOR

Marc E. Smyrl is a research associate at Defense Forecasts, Inc., where he writes on a variety of current economic and political/military issues. Previously he worked as a legislative aide in foreign and defense policy for Senator Gary Hart. He received a B.A. in political science and economics from the University of Denver and a Master of Arts in Law and Diplomacy from Tufts University's Fletcher School of Law and Diplomacy.